Poetry

In the same way that the mindless diamond keeps
one spark of the planet's early fires
trapped forever in its net of ice,
it is not love's later heat that poetry holds,
but the atom of the love that drew it forth
from the silence: so if the bright coal of his voice
suddenly forced, like a bar-room singer's—boastful
with his own huge feeling, or drowned by violins;
but if it yield a steadier light, he knows
the pure verse, when it finally comes, will sound
like a mountain spring, anonymous and serene.
beneath the blue oblivious sky, the water
sings of nothing, not your name, not mine.

Antonio Machado (translated by Don Paterson)

mimesis reveals the mystery of order as a tension between its potential and actual existence

Dalibor Veseley, *Architecture in the Age of Divided Representation: The Question of Creativity in the Shadow of Production*

The young poet... can attain a perfection without much training and experience—a phenomenon hardly matched in painting, sculpture or architecture... *Mnemosyne*, the mother of the muses, is directly transformed into memory, and the poet's means to achieve the transformation is rhythm... a poem, no matter how long it existed as a living spoken word... will eventually be 'made'... written down and transformed into a tangible thing... because remembrance and the gift of recollection, from which all desire for imperishability springs, need tangible things to remind them, lest they perish themselves.

Hannah Arendt, *The Human Condition*

The metaphor with which I have been concerned with is more extended—a double one—in that it involves three terms, a body is like a building and the building in turn is like the world.

Joseph Rykwert, *The Dancing Column: On Order in Architecture*

Lynch mimesis Architects

Artifice
books on architecture

Contents

Introduction
Patrick and Claudia Lynch

... the theory
Of poetry is the theory of life.

Wallace Stevens, *An Ordinary Evening in New Haven*

Mimesis is the physical, rhythmic incarnation of the urgency of the impulses that architecture begins with and echoes with. It is both intensely bodily and also immaterial, like the haunting resonance, Goethe suggested, of a bell that lingers and "evokes harmony".[1]

Architecture begins with dialogue and flourishes in conversations. In this exchange images are transformed from memories into words and drawings via physical gestures, and these in turn are transformed into a built world by intense thought and craft. But this is not the conclusion of the process. The philosopher Jan Patočka describes existence in terms of horizons that we are drawn towards, and for him, inhabitation involves as much imagination and language as it does hunger and desire.[2] For some of us, these are the same thing.

The idea of this book is to acknowledge the importance of what the literary critic Harold Bloom called, in his theory of poetry originally published in 1973, "the anxiety of influence"—a condition that he saw as an "anguished" drive towards originality in young, mostly modern poets.[3] Influence originally meant "in flow" Bloom claims: "to be influenced meant to receive an ethereal fluid flowing in upon one from the stars... a power—divine and moral... in defiance of all that seemed voluntary in one".[4]

As well as revealing something of the physical mimetic processes at play in the work of Lynch Architects, our aim is also to present some examples of influence, showing how past architecture, transformed via imaginative interpretation—what Bloom calls "swerving" or "poetic misreading"—is relevant and useful to an architect working today.

Our references as architects range across time, and in this case are, perhaps obviously, mainly European. The gestures and poises that we mime are always personal, of course, just as we learn a language from our parents—albeit actual or self-consciously adopted ones. But

1 Cited in Martin Heidegger, *Art and Space*, trans Charles H Seibert (*Die Kunst und der Raum*, SG Erker Verlag, St Gallen, 1969): "It is not always necessary that what is true embody itself; it is already enough if spiritually it hovers about and evokes harmony, if it floats through the air like the solemn and friendly sound of a bell."
2 Patočka, Jan, *Body, Community, Language, World*, Open Court Publishing, 1997.
3 Bloom, Harold, *The Anxiety of Influence: A Theory of Poetry*, 1973, Oxford University Press, 1997. In the 2nd edition Bloom refers to "the anguish of contamination" felt by Shakespeare from Marlowe. Bloom describes a series of types of influence (Clinamen or Poetic Misprision; Tessera or Completion and Antithesis; Kenosis or Repetition and Discontinuity; Daemonization or The Counter-Sublime; Askesis or Purgation and Solipsism; and Aprophades or The Return of the Dead). He suggests but does not emphatically declare that "strong" poets risk more, risk themselves, in going beyond selfhood in their work in terms of "emptying out" (Kenosis) of personality, albeit with Messianic overtones. He also suggests a sort of 'daemonic' quality in poetic work that transcends the safety of influence as copying, citing the Biblical example of Adam and Satan in Milton as archetypical of modern poets seeking to invent themselves, whilst acknowledging and, or, rejecting the paternalistic influence of tradition. What is obviously similar, but often unacknowledged by visual artists, is our debt to others, something that Bloom describes as the original influence of art upon our younger selves—what he calls a poem speaking to "the poet in the poet". This means that initial poetic attempts are called forth at first as impersonation, and stylistic imitation often remains exactly simply that. Mature poetics involves risk, and what is at stake is different in every case, but influence remains as at least as important as subjective experiences, if not more so, Bloom suggests: "We need to stop thinking of any poet as an autonomous ego, however solipsistic the strongest of poets might be. Every poet is a being caught up in a dialectical relationship (transference, repetition, error, communication) with another poet or poets." (p 91).
4 Bloom, *The Anxiety of Influence: A Theory of Poetry*, p 26.

Patrick Lynch, *Study Collage for a balcony room on Victoria Street*

the theatrical nature of mimesis means that it remains directly relevant to the public nature of architectural praxis.

For example, the influence of the Ca d'Oro, a sixteenth century house situated on the Grand Canal at Venice, is relevant to us because it presents a decorous facade to an important thoroughfare—a typical situation that we find in cities today. Its deep face mitigates its southerly orientation with a civic aspect, whilst protecting a domestic environment within. It protects both in terms of creating privacy and avoiding asocial autonomy: the stone facade projects a strong identity that enables a private world to exist behind an architectural mask. The deep balcony is an ambiguous threshold, an environmental and psychological buffer between the city and the Ca d'Oro's inhabitants—establishing a symbiotic balance between inner and outer lives. The Ca d'Oro's potential inspiration for architecture today is profound. We hope that its transformation in our work begins to reveal the potent imaginative possibilities inherent in design—not least in avoiding any crudely stylistic sense of imitation.

In Vienna, last summer, one of us for the first time, but it felt like we'd been there together many times before. Like a lot of capital cities, it is like walking around in a film made up of memories almost entirely culled from books and films. It is an odd sensation, like being in a museum of architecture, or one's subconscious gallery of memory images.

This isn't an unusual condition, or emotion. In fact, it bears close comparison to the process of designing, and to those moments when it sometimes feels like you are trying to find the right book, and can only do so by putting out your hand for it as it were: or like tracking down an allusion suggested in a dream. Which suggests that there should surely be some kind of literary theory based on the primacy of images. And there is. It is called architecture.

We once saw the poet, painter and playwright Derek Walcott speaking in London and heard him declare that "poetry is really images, whose power stays with you long after you have forgotten the words of the poem".[5] This suggests to us that architecture might be said to be, essentially, a type of concrete poetry.

5 In conversation at The Queen Elizabeth Hall 25 February 2004. Walcott's *Tiepolo's Hound*, Faber, 2003, considers the reciprocity between landscape and language in the work of Caribbean-French painter Pissarro.

Opposite
Pete Youthed, *Study for a Monument to William Blake*, Undergraduate Unit at London Metropolitan University, 2006–2007, taught by Patrick Lynch, Alun Jones and Karin Templin

Above
Naples Drawings, Intermediate Unit 1, 2002–2003, The Architectural Association, unit masters Andy Houlton, Patrick Lynch and Tony Swannell

Claudia Lynch, *Dream House*

Claudia Lynch, *Marsh View Living Room*

On Mimesis and Type in the Work of Lynch Architects

Alexandra Stara

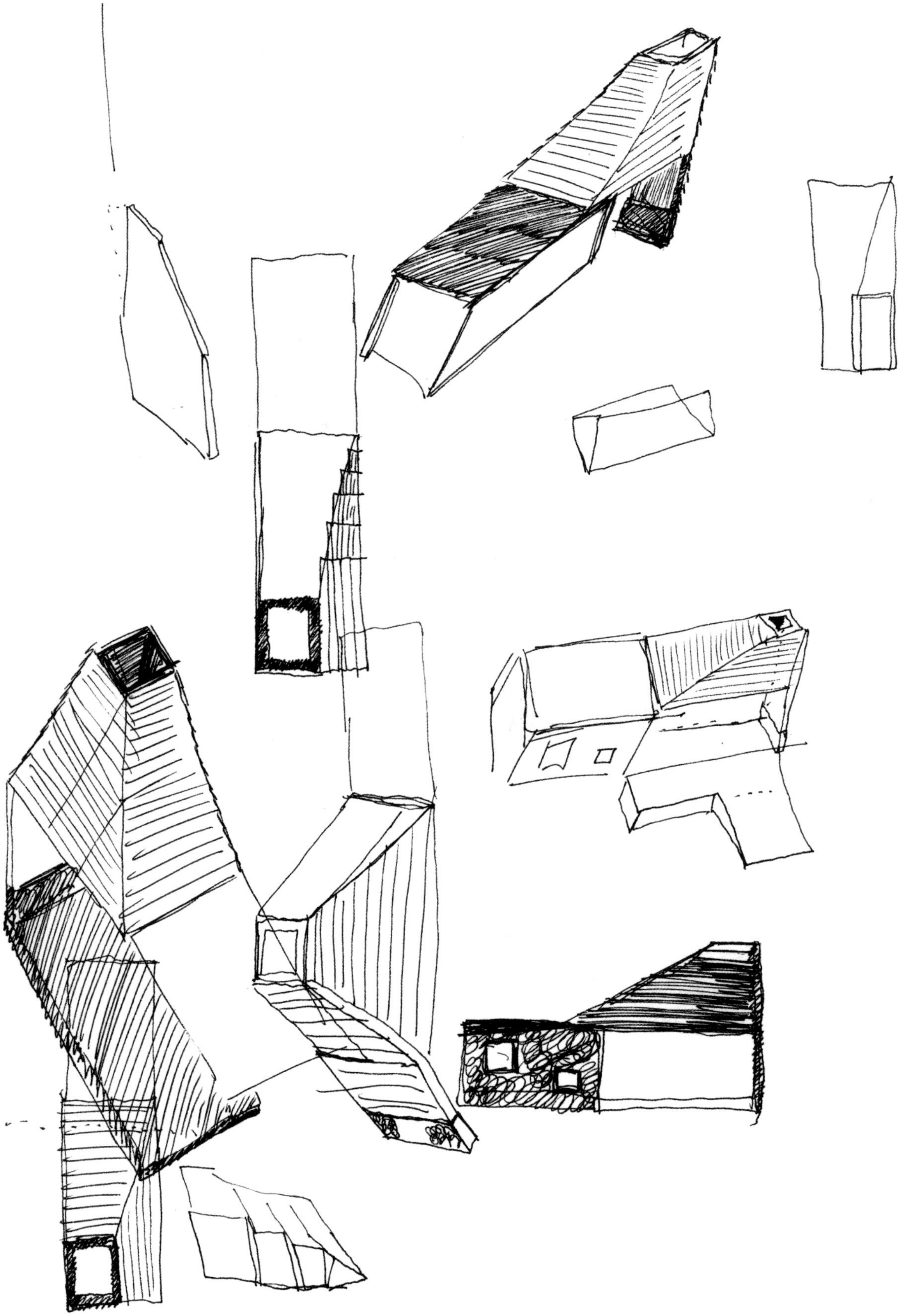

In 415 BC, in Athens, Greece, Euripides staged his latest tragedy, *The Trojan Women*, for the dramatic contest that formed part of the annual Dionysia festival. Set at the end of the Trojan War, the play re-enacted the tragic fate of the royal women of Troy after their city's conquest by the Greeks. Composing one of the most prominent threads of Greek mythology iterated in countless works of poetic representation, the stories of Troy and its predicament would have been familiar to all. As such, they constituted an ideal setting for Euripides to situate his plot in—a plot that had as much to do with that fabled conflict as it did with the war currently raging between the Greek city states themselves. Earlier in the year of the play's staging, Athens had slaughtered the entire male population of Melos and enslaved its women and children because the island refused to take sides in the conflict. Dressing the Melian tragedy with the habits of Troy, Euripides inhabited and renewed myth—the foundation of the Greek polis—while investing the contemporary situation with distance and decorum, rendering it both sharper and more open for engagement with his audience. Although the play did not win the contest, it remains one of the most resonant dramatic works of mankind, able to communicate with contemporary audiences two and a half millennia later, as a live piece of sophisticated theatre, not an archaeological relic or a sentimental one-liner.

But it wasn't Euripides' unbridled creativity that led him to this achievement; it wasn't his unfettered imagination, or his radical innovativeness. Euripides, like several of his fellow tragedians, composed his work through a deep understanding of the conventions of tragedy—a precise dramatic type—as well as the typicality of situations that drama is called to re-enact. He was also, of course, part of a culture that was different from ours, offering considerably clearer—and fewer—pathways between means and ends in human endeavour. Our distance from the ancient Greek world requires critical appreciation so that it might be properly understood. But, to quote Gadamer, "anyone who thinks that art can no longer be adequately grasped using Greek concepts (he means *ancient* Greek) is not thinking in a sufficiently Greek way".[1] In other words, the human condition, whilst deeply historical and therefore subject to degrees of change, is not quite reinvented every morning. Our modern terror of roots and lust for the radical has not changed the fact that we remain *bound*—the etymology of which relates to bonds and boundaries but also to readiness, direction and, quite brilliantly, dress—as in, the act of vesting oneself appropriately in preparation for life's situations.

Lynch Architects have been developing their practice from the outset through serious investment in the continuity of references we call tradition, understanding that the mimetic imagination at work in classical tragedy—and much else since—remains the foundation of meaningful making. Mimesis, properly understood, is creativity, to the extent available to us mortals. Inherent within it is transformation, because "mimesis does not imply a reference to an original as something other than itself, but means that something meaningful is there as itself".[2] Despite its linguistic proximity, imitation, in its contemporary, banalised sense is quite far from what is at stake here, conjuring up images of young gentlemen at their easels competing for the best copy of a Titian in the *Académie*. The open-ended, dialectic relationship inherent in mimesis is closer to analogy, which Paul Ricœur has summarised as a dialogue between Same and Other, holding within it the force of both re-enactment and distancing.[3]

Closer to architecture, what this resonates with is the idea of type, albeit one carefully reconsidered to avoid the many pitfalls it can lead to. Part of the difficulty with typology is its appropriation by postmodernism as a response to the universalism and abstraction

Opposite
Patrick Lynch, *Sketches of Marsh View*

Above
Photographs of Holkham Beach and Burnham Norton Sea Wall

1 Gadamer, Hans-Georg, "Poetry and Mimesis", in *The Relevance of the Beautiful and Other Essays*, Cambridge University Press, 1986, p 122.
2 Gadamer, "Poetry and Mimesis", p 121.
3 Ricœur, Paul, *The Reality of the Historical Past*, Marquette University Press, 1984, p 36.

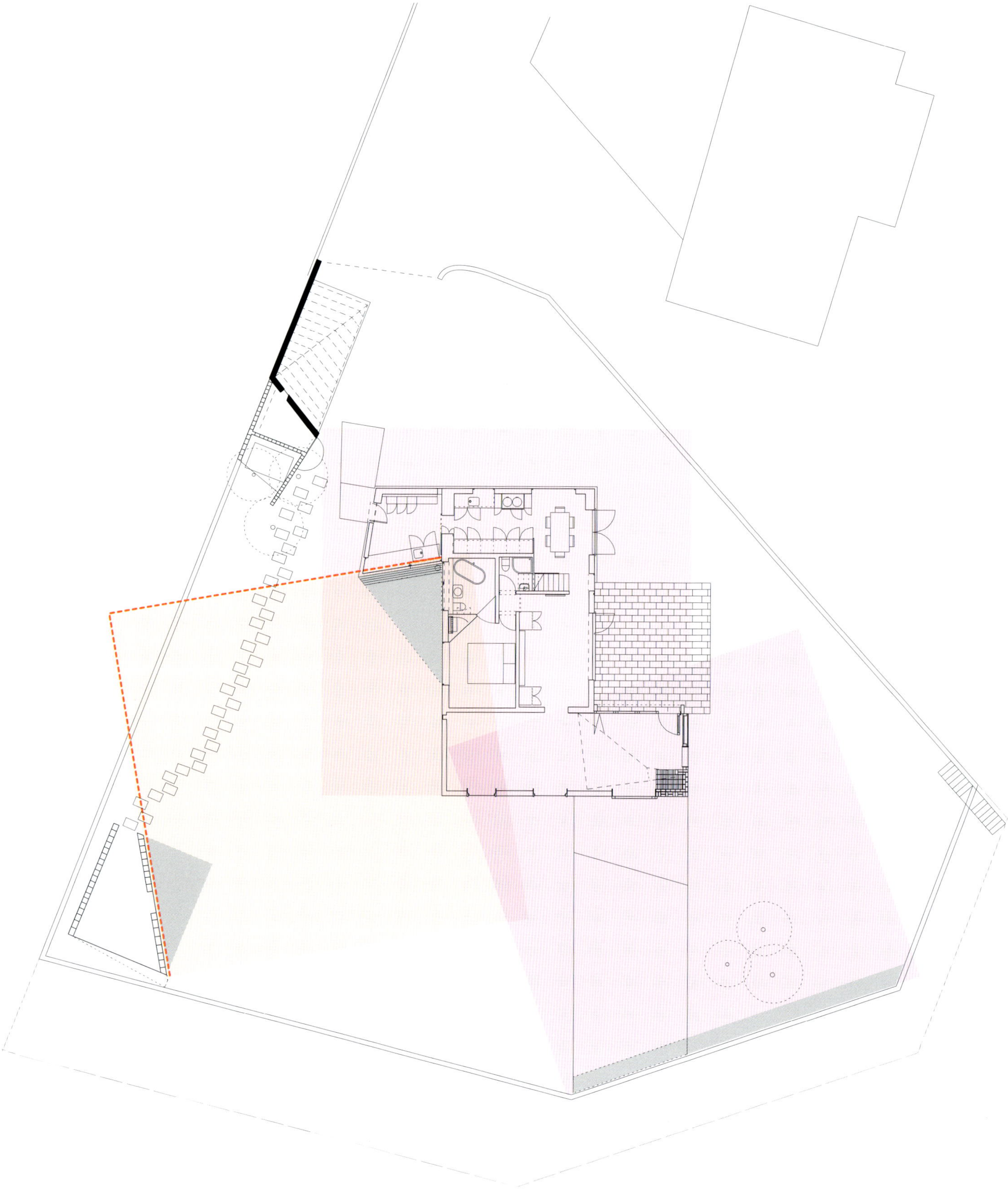

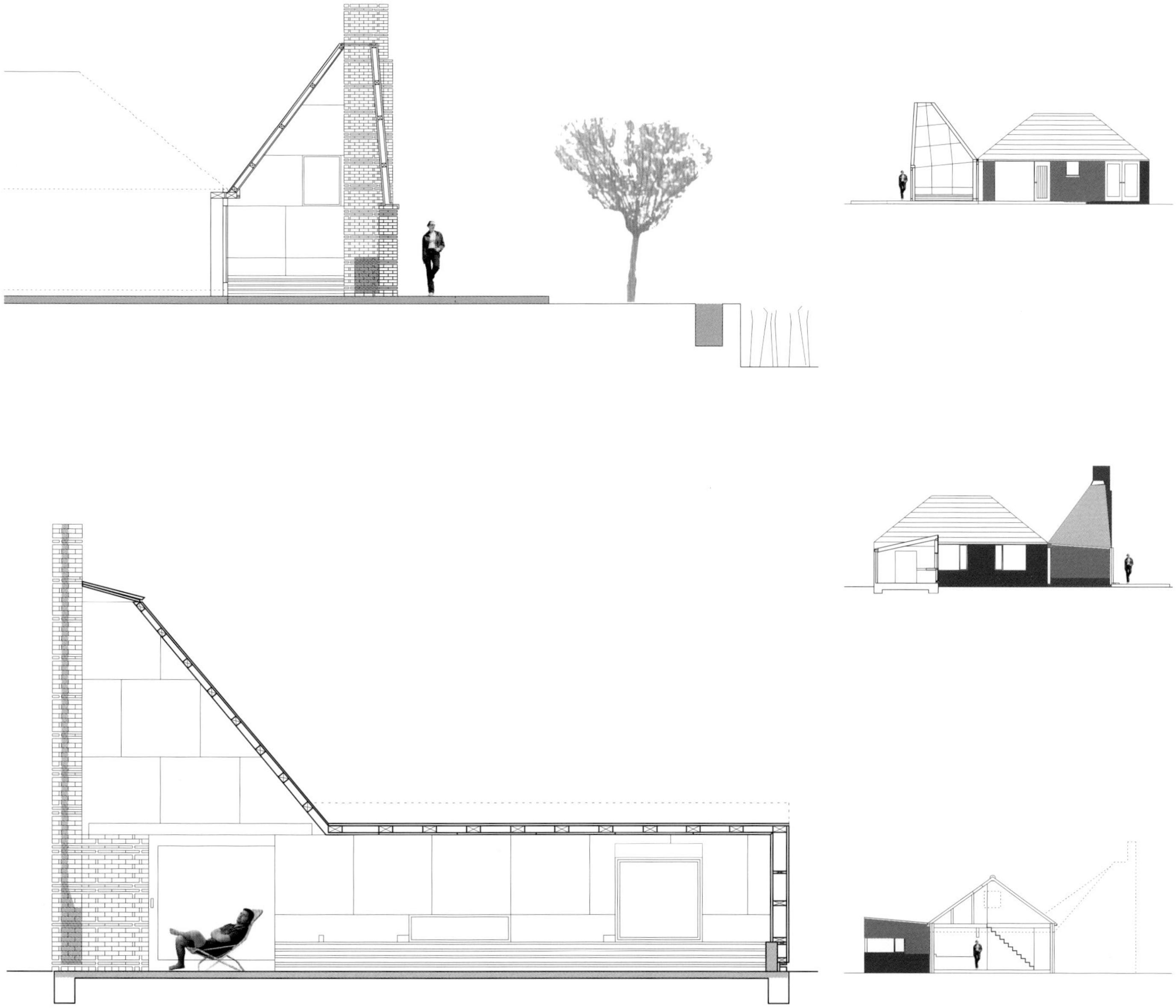

Opposite
Marsh View ground floor plan showing geometric relationships between building fragments and the landscape garden features

Above
Marsh View section drawings

associated with modernism. However, much of postmodernism's relationship to type has been misguided, reducing this rich and dynamic idea to a purely formal structure with an instrumentally conceived relationship to history. Type is not an abstraction or a model to be dumbly copied anymore than mimesis is imitation. As Giulio Argan put it in his seminal re-reading of Quatremère de Quincy: "The word 'type' does not present so much an image of something to be copied or imitated exactly as the idea of an element which should itself serve as a rule for the model."[4] Type is historical, not historicist, and its role is paradigmatic and analogical, offering an interpretative scheme for architecture as poetic act, rather than a mere set of formal choices. Crucial to this understanding of type is that it cannot survive in the realm of abstraction alone, pronounced in a definitive, *Dictionnaire*-like manner. It is, instead, manifested through the embodied reality of building, across but not quite outside the various iterations of formed matter and its modes of inhabitation.

The villa is a type that Lynch Architects have worked with in different contexts, responding and transforming it in often unexpected but always appropriate and enriching ways. Patrick Lynch studied the history of the villa for his Cambridge MPhil dissertation (published as *The Theatricality of the Baroque City*), and the seriousness and detail of his understanding shows clearly in the manner of the practice's architectural gestures.[5]

Marsh View, a holiday home in Norfolk completed in 2003, was Lynch Architects' first substantial built project. Built originally for a textile artist, Alison Mitchell, it sits in a loose scattering of 1950s bungalows at the bottom of a gentle slope. The project required the demolition of an existing bungalow on the site and its partial reconstruction as part of a new composition. Archetypal elements of 'house' are present here—the pitched roof, the chimney—but they are reinterpreted with exaggeration that borders on subversion, being made richer and contingent rather than pared down and clarified. The aim is not destructive—there is no postmodern irony or pastiche here—but a sense of surprise, disquiet, even, alerting us to the referential and expressive depth of the project. The architects have clearly taken great delight elaborating typological references of the leisure home in the countryside—that is, the villa—translated into the local vernacular and appropriately reinterpreted for its modern inhabitants. The villa as type is characterised less by its domestic and more by its social dimension, as well as its relationship to landscape and nature. The combined house and garden offer a repository for art, a symbolic representation of the cosmos, a mediator between nature and artifice, and a setting for the transformation of the mundane into the festive. The client, Alison Mitchell, wrote that Marsh View is extraordinary, "like a stage on which to perform a piece of life itself, if only for a weekend".[6]

The elements composing Marsh View include the main house and various small ponds as well as settings for sculptures by Alison Mitchell's mother Christine Mitchell.[7] A separate studio, a carport and additional landscape features were built in 2008 for the second owners, a doctor and an amateur artist. The architects suggest that they originally thought of the composition of Marsh View as rooms in the landscape, highlighting the importance of the site as a setting for the architectural drama. The theme of reflection is recurrent in the project and the mirror-treated studio cladding, apparently disappearing into the landscape, is one of

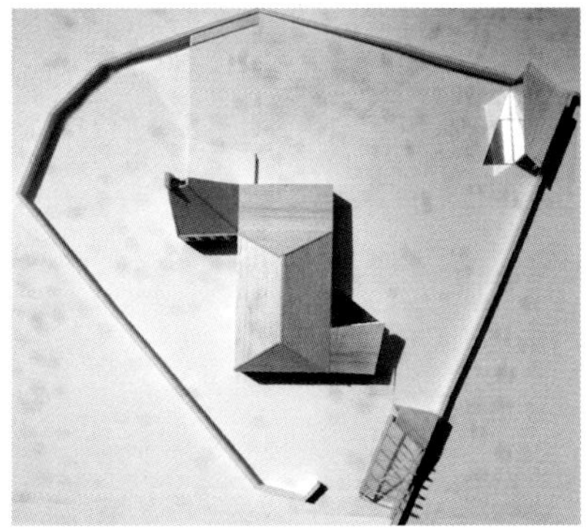

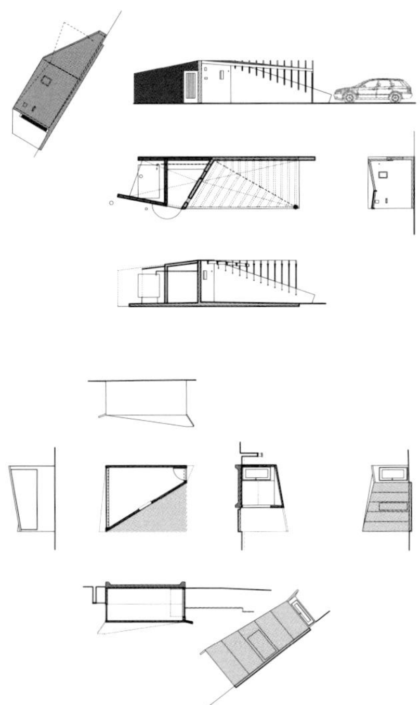

Marsh View aerial photograph showing the extent of a 50-year flood model photograph and plans, and sections of carport and studio

---

4 Argan, Giulio Carlo, "On the typology of architecture", in *Theorizing a New Agenda for Architecture: an anthology of architectural theory 1965–1995*, ed Kate Nesbitt, Princeton University Press, 1995, p 243.
5 Lynch, Patrick, *The Theatricality of The Baroque City*, Dr Müller Verlag, 2011.
6 Cited in Patrick Lynch, "All memory has to be re-imagined: The villa and architectural imagination", *Architectural Research Quarterly*, no 2, vol 9, 2005, p 118.
7 Christine Mitchell taught for a number of years at the art school at Cambridge Polytechnic, and a number of her sculptures can be seen in the gardens of Cambridge Colleges, including work commissioned for the original New Hall (now renamed Murray Edwards College).

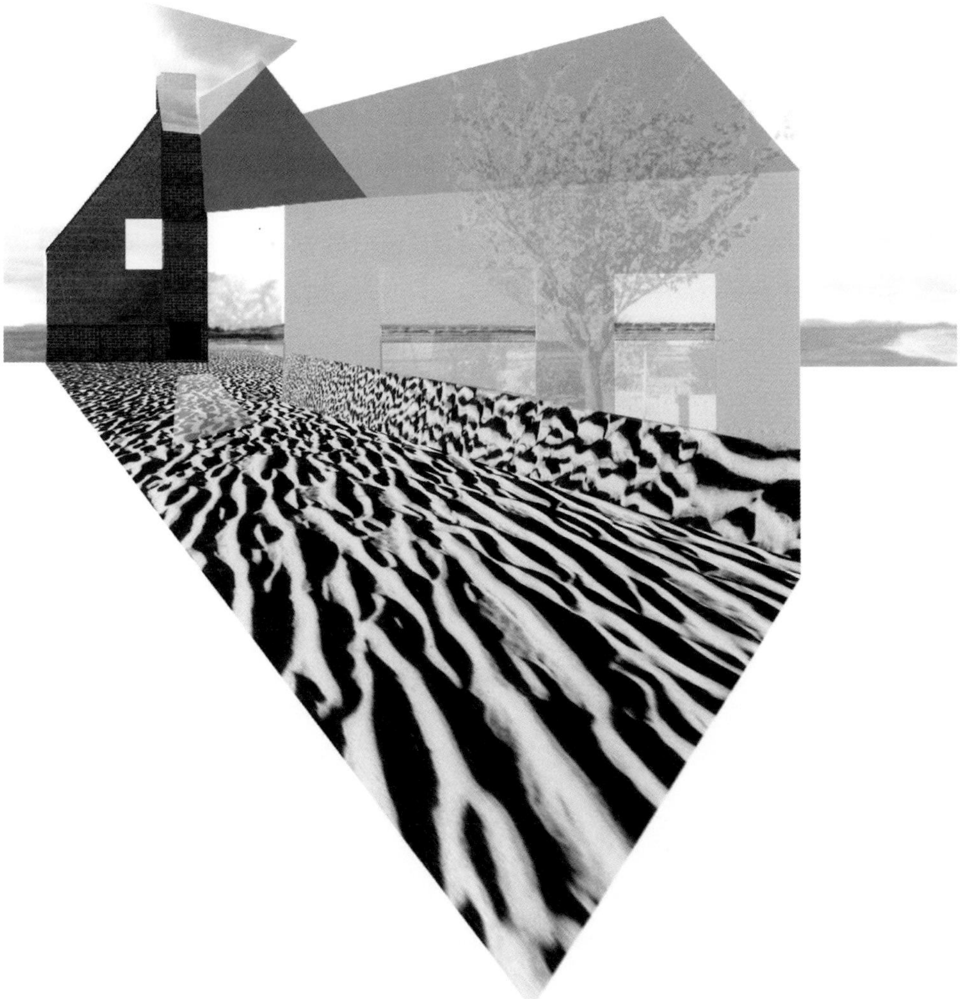

the most prominent of such instances. Dramatically framed views, unexpected angles and surprising spatial articulations abound throughout, manifesting another of Lynch Architects' long standing references, Baroque theatricality. The use of plywood as structural skin internally, the black concrete floor, heated, uniting the volumes of the central enclosure, the exposed concrete, brickwork and reflective glass, are clearly modern tectonic gestures that allude to dimensions of the typology whilst transforming it creatively for its contemporary situation. Rather than just being signified, the tradition of the villa is *taking place* in Marsh View as embodied, inhabited meaning.

A rather different (yet obviously also 'same') iteration of the villa is to be found in Madder Rose, a small commercial art gallery in Clerkenwell, London, completed in 2006, part of a conversion of Georgian terrace houses that includes two apartments. Lynch Architects made no attempt to erase the latent domesticity of the space in favour of abstract neutrality, as is often the case for such a programme, remembering that the origins of the art gallery are domestic. Renaissance villas included a space associated with the entrance—usually a long 'gallery' or sequence of spaces forming part of the introduction to the main salon—where paintings and sculptures would be on display. The villa gallery was an essential manifestation of decorum, situating the family socially and historically. As with the negotiations of existing fabric and uneven topography in Marsh View, Lynch Architects embraced the fragmented,

Marsh View study collage of the double-height living space with models and construction photographs

awkward spatial structure of the existing houses in Madder Rose, seeing it as an opportunity rather than a hindrance. The gallery addresses the works not as disengaged, autonomous apparitions in a space of mere convenience for commercial exchange, but as inhabitants. The architecture invites them to settle in for a while, claiming different corners and setting up different opportunities for engagement with the viewers. There is a corridor, bringing whatever hangs on the wall close up and offering it to us while we are moving; the main 'salon' is a subtly complex room a few steps up, with a deceptive geometry, partly visible from the street and partly hidden, and an intriguing orthogonal box as ceiling hanging between two skylights, which the section shows to be the terrace of the flat above; there is a staircase leading downstairs to the basement exhibition room, which is only revealed once we are halfway down, whilst, immediately above us as we descend, the underbelly of another staircase shapes the ceiling, alluding to yet another aspect of the private world beyond. The resulting sense of surprise emphasises the way we discover things in space, and makes us aware of how we chose to look at something, offering artists and curators a variety of challenges and opportunities to think outside the conventional white cube. Several artists were compelled to make site-specific installations with their work here, responding to the space's palpable invitation to be played with.

Although pervaded by an air of domesticity, Madder Rose is far from mundane. Lynch Architects' well-practised Baroque devices of ambiguity and illusion are employed anew, in good measure. One of the more dramatic gestures is found at the entrance, just behind the glass facade: with the use of reflective glass on the floor, allowing a hint of the gallery's basement office, and mirrors on the side wall and ceiling above, an intense play of degrees of transparency and reflection is effected. The threshold between city and gallery is accentuated as a moment of transition from the everyday to the extraordinary, even as the actual boundary is blurred (and, for once, this frightfully overused expression is precisely applicable). The continuous shadow gap between walls and floor throughout the gallery—one of the subtler moments of conceit at work—becomes particularly effective in the basement. Taking the narrow staircase down from the ground floor and upon turning the corner at the landing, we are surprised by an elegant double-height space, with a window at ground level above us, and a striking black floor, unique to this room. The poured material has a cool, chthonic feel to it, seemingly disappearing under the walls as *ground*. On the hot summer day of the gallery's opening, walking barefoot on it was one of the many unexpected joys of the event. The excavated, shaded quality of this space sets up an interesting juxtaposition with the skylit, elevated salon upstairs.

The success of this imaginatively referential setting for the display of art hinges on Lynch Architects' understanding of the importance of site, as physical manifestation and *situation*. The gallery facade relates to the street decorously, as appropriate to its function, with rather expensive materials and careful detailing, but without ostentation or formal disjunction, responding to the street's Georgian character and its contemporary gentrification. The facade's glass window can be completely opened, introducing a further instance of possible fusion between street world and art world. The other street window allows the observant gallery visitor to catch an intriguing glimpse of Bunhill Row gardens and the historic non-conformists' cemetery, through a narrow perspective along a side street framed by drab social housing and a Victorian school. The neighbourhood of the gallery is London at its eclectic best—from Hawksmoor's St Luke to the Barbican via half-bombed Whitecross Street, with Georgian terraces on one side and council estates on the other—and this view sums it up perfectly.

The apartment directly above the gallery, forms an essential part of the gallery's architectural scheme. The mysterious cube suspended above the skylit exhibition space—a dexterous architectural gesture partly compressing and partly expanding that room, infusing it with a dynamism its proportions would not have otherwise allowed—is revealed as the apartment's

Opposite
Patrick Lynch, Madder Rose Gallery, sketch of the sunken gallery

Above
Collage and model photograph and Christian Cuninghame, Madder Rose Gallery, photograph of the street facade

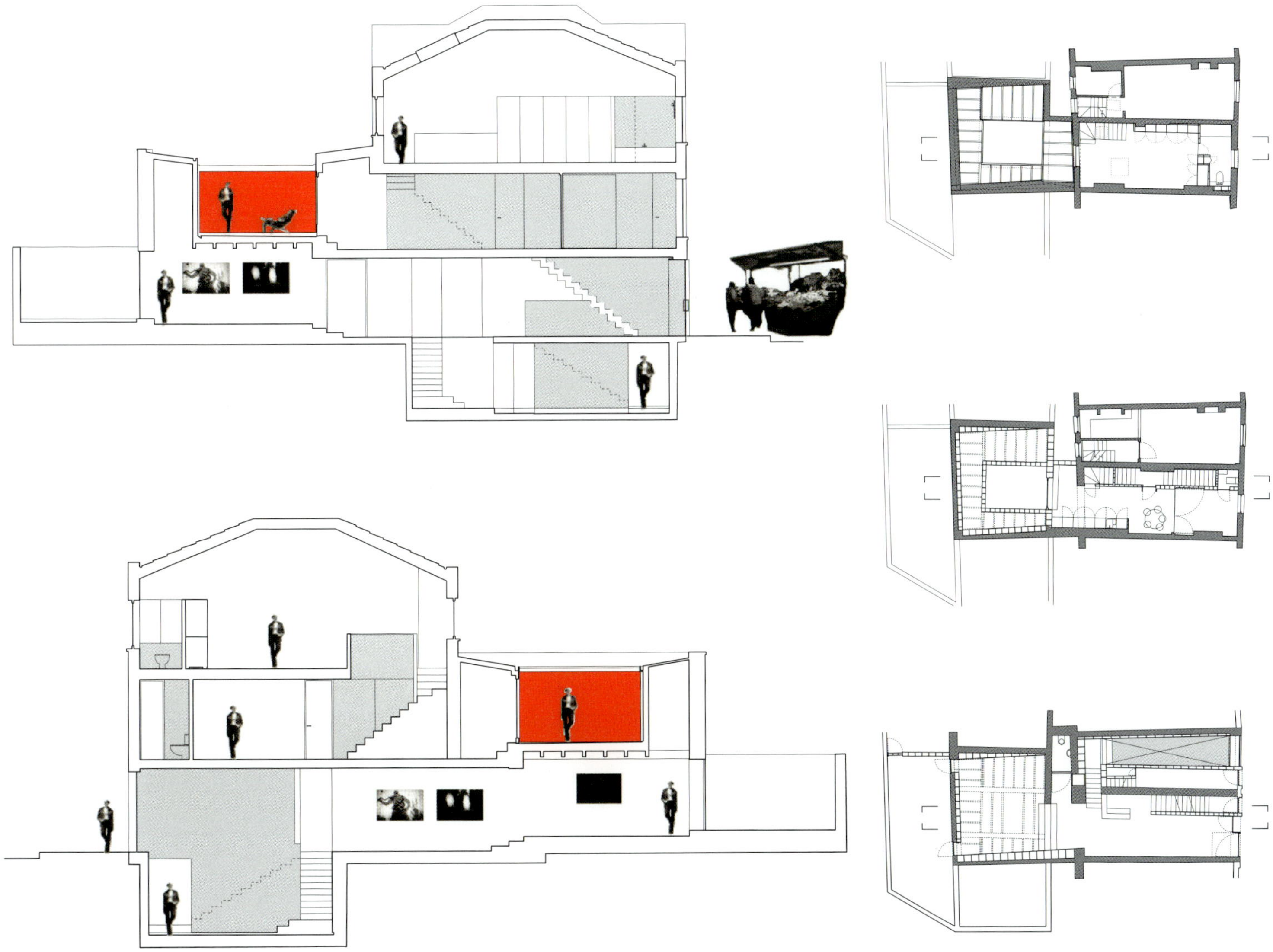

Opposite
Patrick Lynch, Madder Rose Gallery, photograph of gallerists' flat

Above
Madder Rose Gallery, sections and plans

roof terrace. Concluding the long, single space that runs the length of the plot from street front to back yard and comprises all living areas of the flat, the roof terrace is walled in to the height of the interior space. It is a room without a ceiling, painted in the beautiful dark red known as madder rose. The roof terrace and one's approach to it brings to mind the roof top garden room of the Bestegui apartment at Paris by Le Corbusier and its surreal relationship with the Eiffel Tower. While denied full views in this warm, red protected shell, fragments of the London skyline jut above the parapet—the council block just behind, one of the Barbican towers farther away—situating this rather surreal space in its own urban context. In a moment of delightful playfulness, just before stepping out onto the terrace, the architects have placed a mirror on the wall to our right, which reflects the tower to our left, but which we cannot see yet, except in reflection. Composing a piece of city through imaginative play between familiar references and their strange transformation, Lynch Architects have carved an intellectually ambitious and architecturally sophisticated scheme out of the two Georgian houses, with an abundance of optimism for the role of art and artfulness in everyday life.

The typology of the villa in Marsh View and Madder Rose is manifested in an entirely dynamic way, in reciprocity with the reality of the projects' place and time, as continuing idea and ideal of a certain way of living, of art and nature, negotiation and leisure, reflection and playfulness, and the meeting of the everyday with the extraordinary. Patrick Lynch writes about Marsh View, though we could easily extend this comment to the gallery scheme: "These spatial conditions are seen less in terms of fixed functions and more as a fluid series of places for participation within the overall architectural setting."[8] And, I would add, participation in the continuity of history and the shared ground of culture, which allows us to experience the everyday as more than mundane.

Maurice Merleau-Ponty, in his preface to the *Phenomenology of Perception*, writes that: "The world is not what I think, but what I live through", at the same time as: "Because we are in the world, we are condemned to meaning, and we cannot do or say anything without its acquiring a name in history."[9] Mimesis for Lynch Architects is the basis for architecture's continuing relevance, which extends to the building's materiality, construction and mode of inhabitation. Their understanding of type and tectonics is not part of some theoretical framework or abstract method applied to their projects. They are part of the practical wisdom through which they develop their work, situated in an on-going attempt to gauge the appropriate. They constitute a thesis, a stance towards and understanding of architecture as a manifestation of culture with inalienable historical and material dimensions. We are talking, then, about a philosophy of architecture in the proper sense of the word, which distinguishes it from theory because of the former's essential and reciprocal relationship with the real.

The schemes discussed here, and most of the practice's work to date, display an architectural knowingness and a historical and philosophical literacy that a hasty reader of commentaries such as this might mistake for wilful abstruseness. But the crucial dimension of the practice's work is that it doesn't demand a precise deciphering to make sense. The depth of reference is there and can be accessed by the informed visitor to reveal great richness, but it isn't strictly necessary. This isn't conceptualism, where the absence of a theoretical key renders the building impenetrable. Patrick Lynch writes that "the degree to which narrative elements in a villa can be situated within a coherent approach to daily life is the measure by which we judge the efficacy and power of (such a) project". Put otherwise, the work of Lynch Architects makes sense and delights as architecture, which is, in the end (or is it the beginning?) neither text nor image, but something pulled by gravity, and subject to weathering, exactly as we are.

---

8 Patrick Lynch, "All memory has to be re-imagined: The villa and architectural imagination", p 115.
9 Merleau-Ponty, Maurice, *Phenomenology of Perception*, 1962, Routledge, 1992, pp xvi–xvii and xix.

opening times
12-5pm sat

Interview with Patrick and Claudia Lynch and David Evans

David Grandorge

David Grandorge (DG): You speak about the role of philosophy, history and tectonic research in making an authentic architecture, but before that comes the role of the architect, which is discussed imprecisely in academia all the time, and is very difficult to discuss in practice, because people often can't see the wood for the trees. Can you define what you think the role of the architect is now, and has it changed substantially from the time before the expansion of the office? Do you think that understanding has changed over the period?

Patrick Lynch (PL): Claudia defined it very clearly the other week as giving somebody something they can never imagine…

Claudia Lynch (CL): That was actually a quote from Denys Lasdun! Whom I thought defined it really nicely. He said *to be an architect is to give the client on time, and on budget, what he would never be able to dream of*, something like that. I like this definition because it shows it is always important—especially now as we have larger commercial projects—to think about the best way to spend money and to never forget the client's interests, but also, to remember the role of the architect to imagine something, to make something happen that you can't do otherwise, without an architect.

DG: The architect is the only person who can play that role still?

CL: I think they are the only persons who can *lead* that role. I mean, what's fascinating is how big the team is on projects like this, and how it wouldn't be possible without such a large team. But I think you need an architect to bring it all together.

DG: In terms of the other people you bring together to make such a large project—and as with many projects, there is an artist involved—this can be understood as somehow art being at the service of capitalism, pessimistically. But optimistically, it can be seen as an opportunity to inject some generosity into the public realm, through the way a building speaks with its locality. Have there been any of those collaborations, which have been very special to you, in this regard?

PL: I think that the artist is the one member of the design team with whom you can never predict what's going to happen. We've been very, very lucky to be able to work with some artist friends over the years, and in fact we continue to work with them on larger and smaller scale projects. In particular, Rut Blees-Luxemburg's contribution has remained more or less constant, as client, collaborator and critical ally for almost 20 years. Partly this had to do initially with being literally part of a community in Hoxton, and of course most recently her art work will complete and articulate the streetscape at Victoria. Mervyn Rodrigues engineers designed almost all of the structures of our early projects and continue to work on our smaller buildings.

I'm very interested in the role of chance in creativity, and its relationship with order. Cities give order to our lives, spatial and temporal, social and political of course; and whilst the impetus for development projects is at the moment almost always initiated by financial motives, these are usually explicitly and implicitly countered by the corporate interests of the state; and by the decorum of situations represented in a more or less organised fashion by public opinion. Local interest groups and community representation at the level of local inhabitants are often not quite aligned with local businesses, and historic societies often have their own unique perspectives and priorities. I don't think any architect working on anything larger than a house—and often not even then—has at any time in history ever felt that they had a clear and unobstructed path towards the completion of a successful project. Urban order has always reflected the relationship between human beings and others: and if it represents anything it is the resolution of these potential conflicts into an imaginative, useful and sometimes beautiful whole, but even this is never fixed or entirely ever finished. This is because the designer's role in the creation of urban order has always involved not only

Rut Blees-Luxemburg, *London: A Modern Project*

aesthetic or political decisions, but also confrontation with the explicit laws and the implicit structures of society that enable us to function fully as human beings.

This is why philosophy is important for architecture, and why Plato referred constantly to the example of the polis, why the ideal of the city is so bound up with notions of 'the good life'. It is interesting and important to note that Plato is emphatic about the political significance of beauty, since *it is something that is witnessed by all.* This might appear as an unusually archaic notion for a modern architect to hold dear, but it does suggest to us that the contribution of artists working together with architects might offer us a way to recover the possibility of good urban life.

CL: So what the artist does is also a commentary on society, and what the architect does should be a commentary on society, whereas other consultants are sort of more specifically focused on parts of the whole, but not necessarily the articulation of ideas.

PL: Buildings are not particularly good ways to explicitly articulate complex ideas about goodness, criticality, etc. The failure of avant-garde architecture over the past few decades is a symptom of social failure too, I think. I mean, since the deterioration of any sense of common social purpose in most modern design, what Joseph Rykwert calls "Emirates Style" buildings, ie pseudo-sculptural objects surrounded by road engineering, could be said to have occurred not only because architects have attempted to operate directly like artists, but also because they have more or less abandoned faith in the ability of architecture to become an art that *transcends* function. Architecture doesn't become an art form via 'sculptural form' or by avoiding the social and physical complexities of human situations, but by engaging with life as we find it, and responding with something that nobody else could have imagined. Complex projects involve any number of experts or organisations and individuals with specific interests, and yet neither public consultation alone, nor the application of theoretical concepts from other disciplines, seems to have been able to help us overcome our persistent inability to make decent bits of city. Larger projects compel you to engage with national and local policy, and remain meaningful in artistic terms because all buildings, regardless of scale or size, both accommodate and represent the rhythms of the everyday and ritualistic aspects of city life.

Architecture, when it is good, also enables spontaneity to occur. This might be because it has established enough order and enough structure to enable the drama of human life to take place. I believe that the tension between order and chance might be articulated as 'rhythm', both as things you see, within a facade of a building, its physiognomy and armature, and the capacity that this deep threshold has to situate individuals in relationship to civic life. It is a sort of background and foreground setting that can oscillate between implicit and explicit presence. This metamorphic potential establishes and mediates relationships—not only human life, but also between the natural world and urban habitat. The sort of transcendence I'm interested in might be described as a sort of latent animate theatre completed by people and weather. Walter Benjamin begins his essay on the famously theatrical character of Naples describing it as the most catholic of cities, and I remain a cultural catholic in this regard.

If what you might call, after Peter Carl, *the rhythm of situations*, are placed into propitious relationships with each other and with the city, establishing a sort of civic decorum, then the spontaneity of life doesn't occur by chance. It is not something that just happens because it is something that needs prompts, and one way to guide people's sense of the significance of a certain moment in a building, and of a certain building in a particular urban setting, is art.

Art is the thing that elicits highly emotional reactions from us, and artists, when you work with them on architectural projects, have a very, very clear, single minded idea about what they're doing (the ones that we've worked with thankfully) which is the power of art to arrest your consciousness at a certain moment, and to make you extremely conscious of your body, and your perception, not just bodily but also your consciousness.

Above
David Grandorge, *New York I*, 2002

Below
Andy Laurie, Teatrino Salemi
Francesco Venezia

That is, in one sense, very, very similar to the latent and silent role of an architectural project, because it is making you aware of your conditions, and the social context around you as well as the physical world, but also the significance of urban order in particular points in the city. This reciprocity is the topic of my PhD as well as the subject of our continuing projects at Victoria, as well as themes in the smaller houses and the buildings for the National Youth Theatre.

DG: I'd like to go back to this idea of collaboration, just to understand some of the collaborations that have happened recently. And I think as well as artists, this extends to artisans, people who are very specialist in a material research, and so on. You have written about a philosopher as a "drinking friend"; this suggests a bohemian practice, in a positive sense, which is very interesting when it is inserted into the corporate world. An idea of transcendent craft seems to me to be one of the greatest areas for inserting a joy, a material richness into the project, which is somehow, lacking in capitalistic production.

PL: I think it is fair to say that we—as a group of people working together—tend to socialise together, and a lot of our friends are involved in artistic production. This was true as students in Liverpool, and was something I missed as a student at Cambridge, and was a way of living and working that was intensified in Hoxton in the 1990s, where our studio, where we were also living, was unheated and so cold that we spent a lot of time in pubs out of necessity. This was true for a lot of people so one naturally met and made new friends through what appeared to be a bohemian lifestyle. A lot of people were obviously actually working very hard and it is no surprise that they have gone on to be rather successful. So I think whilst we have always been part of a sort a bohemian cultural world, albeit not as artists but certainly as participants in a conversation, you shouldn't mistake this for slacker culture. It has more to do with the strange character of London cultural life where working class pub culture and the art world used to collide and ferment. I know that sounds very pretentious—all architects like to think it about themselves, and of course the counter to this is the business-like nature of an architect's office, our daily professional duties, etc. Nonetheless, I remain convinced of Aristotle's belief that *the purpose of city life is friendship.*

When we won The Young Architect of the Year Award in 2005, Ellis Woodman reported that we'd turned up with "a builder's van full of models", and it was true; the builders—Gordon Bennett and Kevin Walsh—had built seven projects with us one after the other.

My father was a builder, and so I've always felt literally most *at home* on a building site. In our early projects we didn't draw an awful lot of details, we didn't have very much money to spend on fine finishes, but we did have basic knowledge of building techniques. And so a lot of time was spent on the building site, and then obviously negotiations often involve drinking with builders, and you can learn a lot because they can be very, very interesting people. Builders are like architects and like artists, they're often lone wolves; they've decided to set this thing up on their own, and make their own way in life, and yet the work is only possible due to collaboration and sometimes confrontation, and the only way to resolve this is via dialogue, by being sociable and acting as equals. Pubs demand this of you. When you refer explicitly to the law you've failed to maintain the tacit continuity of respect for craft and people that is what really enables you to work successfully in construction. You also need a huge amount of professional and technical and artistic knowledge of course. But what really matters is how you communicate ideas and remain open to other's ideas, as well as how you find a way to stand your ground and to defend ideas.

Often our ideas about architecture come from an idea about construction: so if it is to be a concrete building, naturally you ask yourself what does that mean thermally, in terms of its environmental performance? And so the next question is what does that mean structurally in terms of its expression? And then the next question is not only what have architects done before in these circumstances, but who do you need to work with? And if you're not stupidly

Opposite and above
Sue Bar, Hatton Place, London, EC1, warehouse conversion of a jeweller's workshop into a home. The new concrete ground floor facade opens at weekends when the street is empty of business, extending the kitchen and dining room into the city, creating an "urban room".

arrogant you ask "who knows more about it than I do?" And, if I'm going to realise this idea well, what do I need to learn in the process of doing so? This sort of curiosity exists at every level in the studio—I don't know as much as some of our collaborators of course, and they have their own particular relationships with specific experts. Learning about material culture is one of the most pleasurable parts of being an architect, and I can't understand why certain architects, often of the older generation, deny themselves this heuristic aspect of work.

The interesting and satisfying thing about working on bigger projects is that this sort of relationship with building as craft and talk still continues. For example, once we knew, pretty early on in the design process, that this was what we could afford, we made a big effort to find out about Jura limestone for Kings Gate, and have established some good friendships in Bavaria and London as a result of a profound commitment to learning about the material—and of course to the craft of *baukunst* and *braukunst*!

DG: Going back to the nascent stages of the practice, when you were working at smaller scales—in terms of building, not necessarily in terms of landscape—what was evident to me, on my recent visit to Marsh View, was a very well judged combination of the special and the ordinary, and the ordinary in the building employs everyday builder's materials.

But also in that, in parts, it is typical, and the way of using an almost typical bungalow form, that is wrapped with a processional sequence, to review the landscape, and that very, very ordinary means, making a very special relationship with an extraordinary landscape.

But I was also struck in this building, by things which I have found to be very evident in some of the strongest architecture I've been privileged to visit; evidence of the uncanny. That there is something, to use the German, *unheimlich*, unhomely, which is necessary to understand a homeliness in that environment.

I think this is accentuated because it is a holiday home, so the idea of the entrance through a study, into this cave, with a black poured resin floor, holding the sky: some incredible moments of spatial disturbance. These strong ideas, which you can really feel, become authentic, in these small scale projects.

Do you think during your journey to working and designing a small piece of city, that there is still any way that you've been particularly able to introduce that form of spatial disturbance, or ambiguity, in the urban realm?

PL: Marsh View is a villa, which is to say a holiday house, and villas traditionally are places to engage with the natural world through the filter of architecture, and that filter can extend to become garden architecture, pavilions, ha-has, bosco-like woods, caves, grottos, etc. The theatrical aspects of Baroque villas and urban gardens was the subject of my Master

Opposite and above
Morley von Sternberg, Greenwood Road

of Philosophy dissertation at Cambridge with Dalibor Vesely: and so, when I got this site in Norfolk, which was on the edge of human habitat, with a marsh beyond it, the banal aspects of it didn't offend me, because I could see that the whole point of the villa is to move you from the mundane towards something sublime.

This extreme juxtaposition is what gives you distortion, and all we had to do is play the comfort aspects up, and the large scale of the landscape would create a powerful juxtaposition. That's saying it retrospectively of course, as if reading and designing are seamless parts of creativity, as if I had the theory for it. It wasn't, it was just that I knew things about what a villa was supposed to do. But it was very much a project of surprises, and discoveries, because it was made through making models and making images, and talking about ideas, instinct and reactions to one's perceptions with the client, who was a very sensitive and powerfully creative textile artist.

One very basic idea is that the bungalow we started with—that we knocked down, ripped apart and rebuilt—was basically a cube, and the land around it was undefined. By distorting and fragmenting the morphology of the built form, the landscape became the solid, inverting the original condition. So if you like the patio to the southwest now feels like a volumetric cube, and the building reads as a series of fragments, so it inverts the relationship between the built object and the ground. So the ground becomes like a volume, it feels like a room.

Opposite
Morley von Sternberg, Greenwood Road

Above
Chris Gascoigne, Greenwood Road

Now that is carried out through devices of re-modelling the form of the building, and registering the volumetric form of the space that's a result of it. The basic devices of composition that occur on Victoria Street are almost the same, in that the previous building that we knocked down was also an introverted object building, and the ground around it had no definition as a consequence. The use of mirrored geometry in the plan-form, for example, was done in order to create a strong volume between the two buildings. It also creates a perspectival sense of enclosure, which is perhaps why the landscape architects Vogt describe the space between the two buildings as being like a Baroque dining room.

We've also registered the horizon of the space very clearly, so that the volume of the public realm feels like an urban room; not just a cliché of one, but a space that you can eat in. The intense rhythm of columns and the repetition and exaggeration of soffits will make clear, I hope, our debt to Baroque urban projects. And by applying mirrors to the ceiling—which you haven't seen yet—when they are built, will, I think, enable an interested critic to read a very clear relationship between our work at Victoria Street and Marsh View. The purpose of this in both cases is to emphasise a certain *Baroque unity of the arts* of landscape, art works and architecture, and to intensify your experience of time passing, other people, your own situation in relation to these phenomena. The intention is also to amplify a certain ambiguity between what Herman Bauer called *seeming and being*. Bauer and Vesely's teacher, Hans Sedlmayr, commented favourably on "the zone of ambiguity between architecture, stucco and painting" at the head of columns in Baroque interiors, and I remain committed to trying to retain this spatial ambiguity in our buildings today. It is a sort of 'modern Baroque', spatially-driven architecture that one sees in the work of Távora, Moretti, Aalto, Siza, Coderch—and arguably also in Lewerentz and Asplund's projects too.

DG: The use of mirrors is extensive at Marsh View, both from inside—holding the landscape, in the bathroom to the master bedroom. But also in the pavilion, in and on the skin of the studio—resulting in the building's ability to not only hold the landscape on the facade, but to dissolve the building with the landscape. I've seen it in very sharp spring evening light. I would love to see it in mist, an apparition, in the landscape.... These devices, these visual distortions seem to me to be the key to your extended research about the Baroque, and its relevance to a contemporary practice. It involves both visual distortion, and attenuation. Can we also talk about the role of mathematics?

PL: Much of what we do as architects involves working with one's body, working with one's hands, making models and making images, and for us it is a very physical process. But in an office building for example, in the main, everything is either curtailed by the site, which most people build up to, or by the geometric order that comes from a 12 x 9 metre column grid, which is the optimum size economically—in either steel or concrete—to achieve certain spans. Oddly though, when you map onto that grid travel distances, and accept the guide that the parameter of solar and civic orientation give you, there are certain geometrical figures that appear and reappear in even the humblest workplace.

DG: Underground car parks, for example.

PL: Well, below Kings Gate, there is an underground car park, which entails, ideally, a certain spatial structure, and then above ground there are other ideal spatial divisions for residential use, which means in simple terms that they are not the same structural grid. But an architect needs to resolve both structural systems somehow at ground level if our cities are to have any hope of becoming liveable places again.

DG: I sense an enjoyment of engaging with some of the rules of commercial outcome.

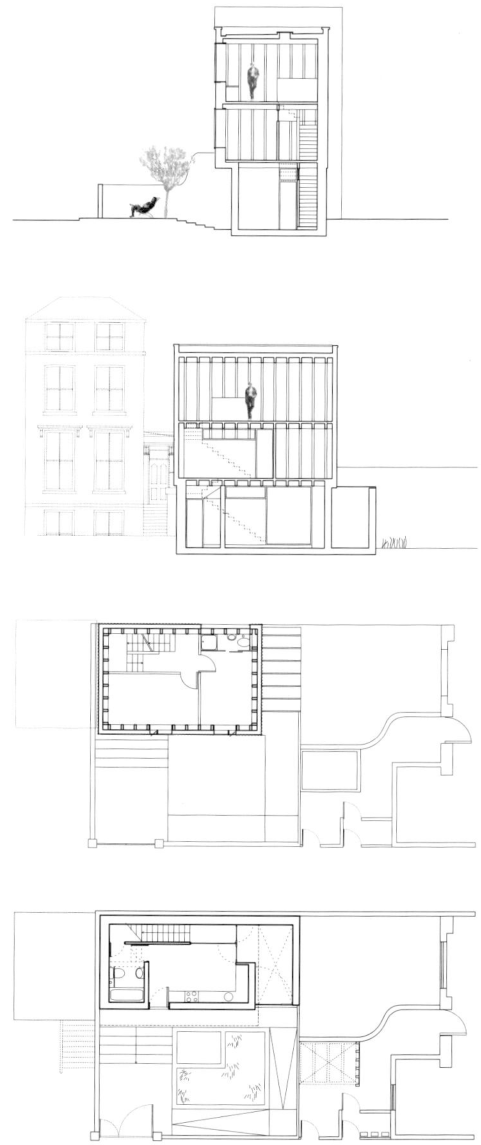

Ground, first floor plan and sections of Greenwood Road House, London, E8

CL: But it is also what you said about chance. I think if you just start with chance, it is just arbitrary and pointless, but if you set up a structure, you know, a logic and a structure, then chance comes into it. But there also seems to be a tradition for structural engineers to, or to try to, make things as slim as possible. If you've worked with older structural engineers, like Sam Price, you would always hear how structure could be half the size, and these days it is quite difficult sometimes, to get them to work in the same way. So the stone columns on the facade of Kings Gate are the thinnest they can be, 16 centimetres wide, and they play a role in the environmental and spatial character and performance of the building as well as its decorum.

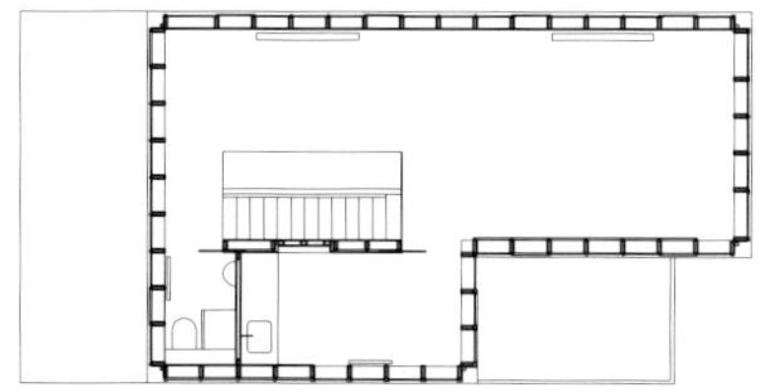

DG: You have stated quite specifically an interest in the structure of space.

PL: Well, in this instance, we didn't conceive of this facade as a structure in load-bearing terms. We conceived of it as a solar screen, an environmental screen, and therefore the thinnest it can get, to hold itself up, is 16 centimetres, to enable us to put tie rods through it, to create tension within the stone. Now, arguably, that's what Mies van der Rohe was doing; using the image of structure to structure space to the extent that his buildings become something like archetypes. So the geometrical, proportional relationships of things to each other is what he was fundamentally interested in. What he became proficient at was understanding the modern steel industry, which was internationalising proportional relationships along lengths and heights and depths of things. And so my sense was that he knew that if this was how he was going to have to build, then he needed to work out how to build well like this. The question remains how to transcend necessity.

Mies van der Rohe is a really important architect for all of us, and of course, if you're going to be doing office buildings, then you need to be looking at him, because he's arguably the first person to turn them into works of art. Against this of course you need to keep Adler and Sullivan's work on the horizon too, as they maintained a strong sense of the role of ornament in architectural facades as well as the ornamental character of large buildings in terms of their role in civic settings. In both cases, early modern architecture had not yet adapted itself to the parameters of ecological comfort, and the next task seems to be to try to engage modern systematic building types with the city; and to enable the individual occupier to exercise a degree of autonomy in terms of their access to fresh air and sunlight, etc. This is why the systems of analysis that involve costs, comfort and efficiency require some degree of scientific knowledge: not only of the mathematics of geometry, but of the principles of physics. This 'parametric architecture', to refer to its originator, Luigi Moretti, would not involve the inappropriate use of pseudo-scientific metaphors relating to form—which are really just examples of inept literary tendencies amongst architects—but appreciation of the broader parameters that influence the design of buildings including their physiognomy and their civic qualities, as well as the role of thermodynamics in terms of comfort and pleasure.

DG: We should bring David into the discussion now. Is this an issue of optimisation? One assumes that because engineers calculate, they would be better at this than architects, but, as you've been arguing—that through a process understanding many processes, ie how long it takes to build the structural stone facade, time, money, etc, you're in a better position to enable optimisation. Was that there, with any clarity, in any of the early processes?

David Evans: It was definitely in it, because we were trying to achieve several things at the same time.

We see a link to Mies' work in many ways. So, the external skin is doing two things, it is acting as a moderator ie it is acting as a facade, but at the same time, it is expressing—where appropriate—the structure: it is not actually the structure, because like with Mies the I-beam on the front of it is just part of the facade at Lake Shore Drive.

So, we were doing a combination of those things to differing extents in the facades of The Zig Zag Building and in Kings Gate, and because of the release of it from being

Plan of new rooftop level of Lynch Architects old studio and house, Hoxton Street, London, N1

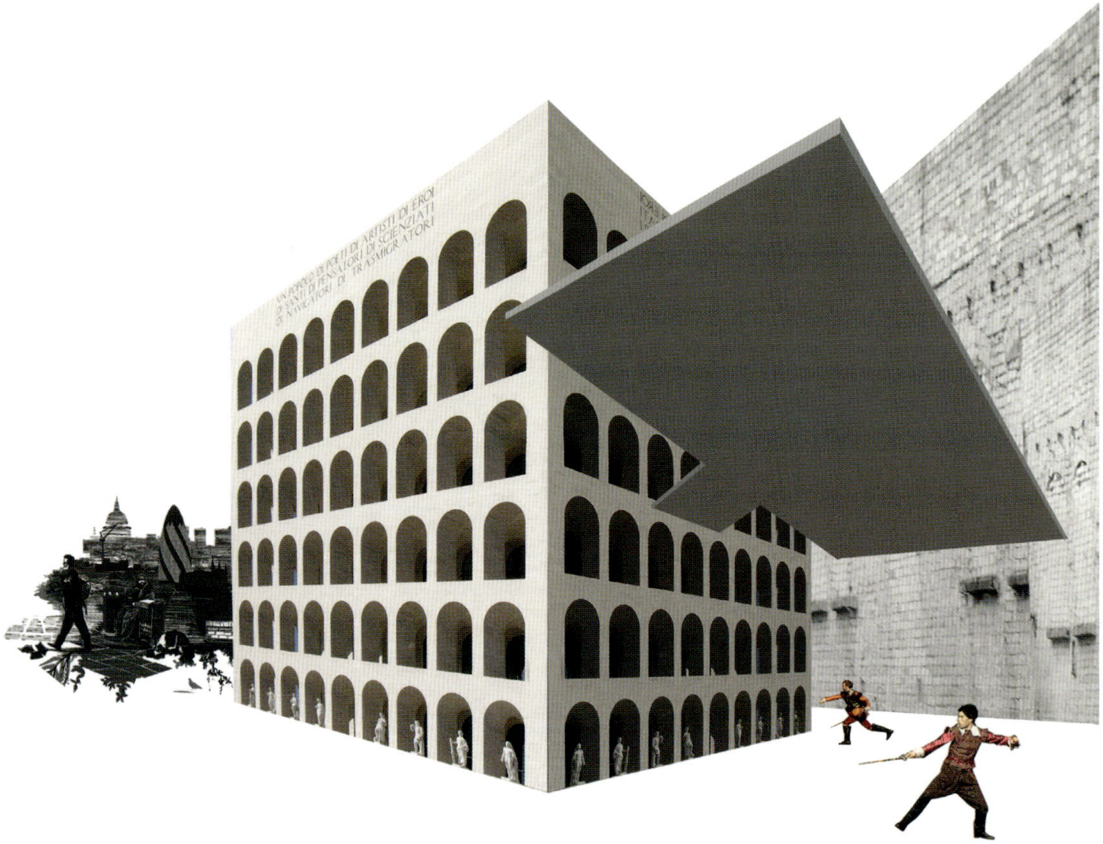
UN POPOLO DI POETI DI ARTISTI DI EROI
DI SANTI DI PENSATORI DI SCIENZIATI
DI NAVIGATORI DI TRASMIGRATORI

an explicit structural element we could get the thinness that we were after. Because what we were trying to play against was the thinness of the structural elements, stone being a structural one, giving it a vertical elegance, and yet almost doing the reverse down at the ground floor level, where most people favour butt-jointed glass with a mastic joint, there we're over-sizing, and making stainless steel, and huge 400 millimetre thick aluminium fins: inverting modernist conventions. Our aluminium cladding system is thicker than our stone, so there's a play going on, because they're not structural elements. Paddy calls this Baroque, I think it is more Mannerist.

It is a series of hierarchies. So The Zig Zag Building is a series, it is three bays. These bays then push inward so that they're in two halves, and then it is organised that each floor level has got a certain amount of fins, and then there's N plus one, N plus two, working through it, so that's a finite hierarchy within that. Behind that, there's a curtain wall module for the internal planning grid, which is recessive, but important to the inside face, rather more than the outside face.

PL: So we have articulated the structure of the building, as David was alluding to, in the scale of the building in 12-metre bays, but the outside does one thing, because it addresses the sun and the street, and the inside glazing module relates to the ceiling grid and the inside of the building.

So one of the dilemmas of modernism, which postmodernist architects have tried to get over, is to say the inside and the outside are completely different, they should have no relationship to each other: and one problem with modernism, which lurks and lingers still, is people say no, it is actually the same, they need to be exactly the same.

But what we think is that the inside is affected by the outside, and the outside is affected by the inside, and that's where you get these layers that we're talking about, which are properly spatial, therefore for us they're properly architectural, as opposed to just being form or sculpture which fulfils no function, and thus is vulnerable—in a capitalistic situation to being cut from the budget.

When they fulfil environmental purposes, ie they have to do with energy conservation, thus saving money, you find that that adds a layer, as it were, of reason to it, which other members of the design team, including the cost consultant, and the contractor, can understand. So unlike Mies, who made these beautiful perfect things but relied upon air conditioning systems, what we've been looking to try and do, very deliberately, is to develop an aesthetics of green architecture.

Opposite and above
Studies for the National Youth Theatre

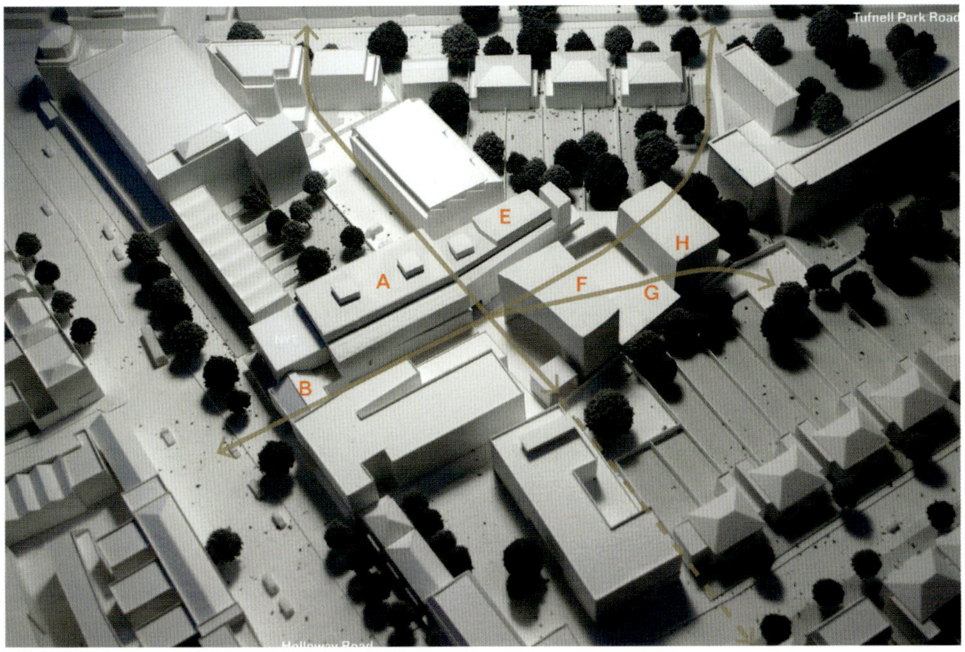

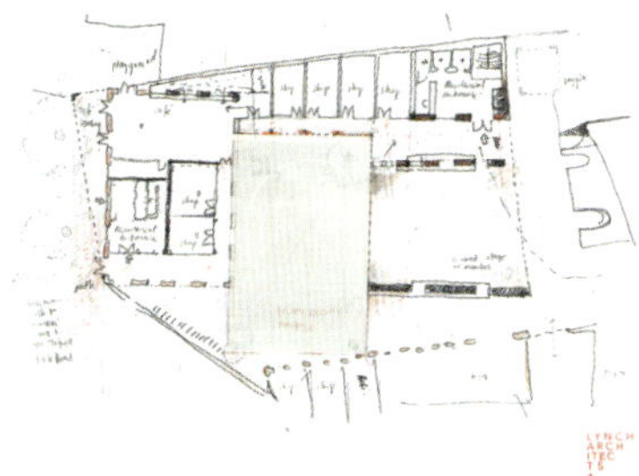

CL: Structure is space, and structure is form. Moretti was interested in the environmental parameters, the structural parameters, the cost parameters, and then because he's building in Rome and Milan, the architectural parameters of decorum, of what you can do, what fits into a city, but both proclaims its modernity and isn't ignoring the tradition of tectonics in architecture, which has informed the articulation of almost all buildings. His influence is clear I think in our recent work at Victoria as well as in our roof top extension on Hoxton Street and in the green-oak framed house on Grenwood Road, also in Hackney.

PL: So the aspect of ornament that we're striving for isn't directly representational of the history of architecture, ie it doesn't look like a Renaissance building. The natural world is present in our buildings, but it is present as shadows, as reflections, as people, and as a proportion ie mathematical ornament, which relates to the scale of your body and relates the building to the city. Obviously, we would like to think that it is palpably perceptible visually, and that it gives you pleasure, makes you think, and can even make you smile.

The philosopher Karsten Harries claims that what we need today is a post-postmodern architecture. I realise that it is stupid to say we are trying to do that. But I think it is true that the contemporary versions of postmodernism and super-modernism that we see some architects indulge in today—with their ignorance of the role of physics and of everyday life in architecture—is ruining our cities.

One fetishises the future, the other one fetishises the past: neither seems to be a very philosophical way of going about being in the world today.

DG: This would be a useful moment to discuss the idea of typological relationship to the office's production. Type as thinking about historical typology, functional typology, thinking of formal typologies, and maybe even an idea of a cosmological type. How have you understood what part, what aspect of typology has been particular to the design processes of the office? For instance, Peter Carl understands typological design as the ability to take something out of the flux of reality, to analyse it in itself, and then to push it back into that messy situation. The possibility for me therefore, is an authenticity beyond the projects contingencies and context, whether they be programme, economic, physical qualities of place.

Opposite
Forbes Massie, collage of The National Youth Theatre and Mercers Road masterplan

Above
The National Youth Theatre, model photograph and sketches

PL: In his book on the villa, James Ackerman very perceptively claims the villa is not a type: it is a state of mind, it is a certain attitude towards a relationship between an actual world and an imaginative territory and a city, where it sits at the cusp of, and mediates. And therefore villas can be lots of different types, in terms of planned form. But certain critics have said that what we were doing in our earlier projects was inventing new types, which then people just started copying.

DG: But there is also a strong early invention at Marsh View that resonates in the world there. There's a lyricism to the form, which resonates with people who enjoy exploring the formal qualities of a building in landscape, which one can understand, that idea of a profile of the investigation.

PL: Yet I think there's a difference between mimesis and copying, which obviously this book is about. Artistic work involves a physical relationship between thinking and doing: it has to do with how you learn to play football, how you learn to dance, or you learn to act, and it is fundamentally I think architectural… the way in which you learn to draw, and you learn to make models is mimetic. I mean, you don't watch other people doing it, but you get the sense, you know, in your body, when it is coming together. In contrast, I think that there is a certain disinterested aspect to typological design, a pseudo-aesthetic, effete copying of other people's creativity, which is rife in the profession. I think all good creative work *tends towards* form, but it doesn't start with form. I mean, there is a philosophical point, one that Plato made, that artistic work is a type of poetics that tends towards ideas, ie towards *eidos*—which is where we get the word 'concept' or 'image' or 'form' from. All mathematical work, all philosophical work, all musical work, all painting, is tending towards form: it is tending towards conclusion and being finished, and being perfect. But by definition it is work, and so doesn't start from its conclusion.

Now that might mean that you finish a project before it is perfect, so that its typical qualities can be inferred, and people can fill the gaps in themselves. My problem with typological based design is that it is a pseudo-science of memory, and of course memory is not scientific, it is something which is active and alive: and the spontaneity of design draws on in it when dialogue is involved.

But this is the thing, because what typology relates to I think is context and decorum, ie that it is an important building and therefore its architectural character changes, it becomes a purer type, and thus it becomes significantly recognisable. This might mean that one can talk about site typologies as much as building programmes exhibiting complexity and requiring a counterpoint, a degree of clarification and intensification. On the other hand, certain situations are so banal that a degree of complexity in formal and spatial terms can create the impression of a certain kind of historical continuity and layered urban depth. You encounter so many sorts of different combinations of sites and briefs as an architect that it would be foolish to approach design with pre-conceived intentions I believe. Having said that, I think that it is clear that we do have an inclination towards a certain latent theatricality. The silent character of architecture is capable of transformation by use. Hans-Georg Gadamer refers to this as a quality as "festive calm". It is probably most evident at Marsh View and in our work for The National Youth Theatre. In both cases the echoes or memories of types set in play the possibility for people's playful participation with the architecture, whilst retaining a certain distance. I think that a certain melancholic withdrawal is a suitable atmosphere in this case, as the architecture is really a backdrop for fun.

Aalto is such a powerful, important architect because he didn't disregard complexity, but was able to synthesise it in such a way that his buildings have this, Claudia said, *resonant quality*, where you recognise something in them that transcends the immediate reference. And so it appears both fresh and part of a tradition at once. This is what I think we would all agree in this room, represents living culture.

Just before Dalibor died, he gave a talk at Eric Parry's office in which he said one thing that shocked me: "if you are intervening in the city, and you don't leave it better than you

found it, and you disrupt all the continuities and discontinuities that you find there, you are not doing creativity, you are just doing production".

That means, I think, that trying to misapply something that you have cribbed from the past, trying to force it, shoehorn it into a situation, has as disastrous effects upon the city as unmediated shape-making: because both just rinse out the complexity of a situation misapplying a sort of pseudo-complexity or simplicity upon a design, before the idea has fully transformed itself, and evolved into typicality, evolved into an image or a form.

DG: Dalibor's idea of mimesis as decorum… it seems to me to that there is an issue here, which is common to looking at continuity as language, as well as continuity in the city… there is also a nostalgia there somewhat, that when the word was conceived of in its original meaning, that the world was somehow better than it is now.

PL: I think all three of us here share a deep respect for language. We all strive to write clearly, to communicate with each other and with people in the office very clearly, and you find that you can get very frustrated, as an architect, when you're dealing with people who don't do that.

Now most people wouldn't necessarily use the word decorum, they would say *it fits*. But as Dalibor points out, that's the original meaning of it, the etymological root of the word 'decorum', as Vitruvius translates it, doesn't originally mean anything more than what is appropriate, which is *prepon* in Greek.

Of course decorum then takes on all sorts of meanings, which we ascribe today in society as being about being old fashioned or conservative, or passive, or reactionary. But what it actually means is to be *appropriate*. I don't think this is in any way nostalgic as it concerns what is right and just today; it is actually to be critical and to be political, because most architecture today doesn't seem to stem from the idea that you should leave the city a better place than you found it. The opposite of acting appropriately seems to stem from the idea that one should be allowed to do exactly what one wants, because that's an expression of freedom. In fact, it is a sort of tyranny of a particular kind of thinking on the city. You only need to think about ecological issues to realise that doing what you want isn't necessarily always a good thing, and that doing what is appropriate entails thinking about what the right thing to do might be. I'm convinced that it is not a random phenomenon that the concept of what is appropriate enters everyday language via architectural discourse, and even if we're not always aware of it in the profession, it remains a strong aspect of the way in which buildings are discussed in everyday life. Wittgenstein believed that one should "look for the meaning in use", and this is our belief too.

Study for National Youth Theatre site, Holloway Road

Civic Architecture

Patrick Lynch

RA
RA
RA

It is this closeness to living recollection that enables the poem to remain, to retain its durability, outside the printed or the written page, and though the 'quality' of a poem may be subject to a variety of standards its 'memorability' will inevitably determine its durability, that is, its chance to be permanently fixed in the recollection of humanity.

Hannah Arendt, *The Human Condition*

The City of Westminster is home to a number of the most important and impressive buildings in England, and is the setting for most of the rituals and ceremonies that we associate with civic society. The architecture of Westminster represents this civic culture, it also embodies and situates it, and in many ways the City of Westminster is a stage for the drama of civic life. The facades of its buildings act as thresholds for this urban theatre, inviting participation and also indicating, through the presence of sculptures, an ideal of public life. This extreme theatricality is characterised also by porticos that open onto courts, and by passages defined by the silhouettes of towers. You find at once the presence of the background in the faces of the major public buildings on Piccadilly, and also the presence of the foreground in the almost secret-seeming character of the hinterland of Victoria. The contrast between the porous and ornamental character of the buildings in Piccadilly and the impenetrable and mute 1960s facades along Victoria Street is the subject of a series of photographs by David Grandorge made from between 2010 and 2014 for the exhibition Civic Architecture, which was held at The Building Centre in London between November and December 2014. Some of the images also appeared in Lynch Architects' contribution to the Venice Architecture Biennale in 2012.

David's photographs also formed part of a film that recorded an interview with Joseph Rykwert in which he discussed the background to the writing of *The Idea of a Town* in the 1950s, and the continued dominance of traffic engineering in the design of new cities today. Dalibor Vesely discussed the introduction of railway engineering into nineteenth century London and Paris, and the continued relevance of ornament and decorum in the creation of civic architecture today. The extreme contrast between the tradition of urbanity represented by the eighteenth and nineteenth century buildings and the impoverished character of the city made by the twentieth century facades could not be clearer. This rift is something that our projects seek to address in terms of emphasising the civic character of architecture.

"Civic" is the transformation of play into structure (laws, rituals, etc), and also the transformation of natural conditions into ornament, ie decorum. This is why we can talk of the decorum of people, costumes, buildings and situations, etc. Decorum in architecture concerns, therefore, not only the facade but also the disposition of spatial situations and the relationships between these parts and the whole, the immediate context, ecology, etc.

"Civic" is a term traditionally associated with Renaissance Florence, and in particular with its use by Hans Baron. Baron uses the term "Civic Humanism" to define and distinguish between the Medieval emphasis upon poverty as grace in Franciscan and Dominican theology, and the proto-modern (neo-Aristotelian and neo-Platonic) world of Ficino, Bruno, Petrarch and Alberti. Of course, we recognise that Petrarch was once a poet, philosopher and gardener, and that Alberti was a priest, philosopher and architect. These factors define the essence of Renaissance Man. Civic Humanism was the expression of this 'tradition'—it was possible at this point in history to lead a contemplative and an active life, Alberti argued, to be at once engaged in city life in a generous and imaginative way, without being a slave to committees or to greed. What we now call "modern" is also

Opposite
David Grandorge, Burlington House

Above
Lynch Architects, Inhabitable Models exhibition, Venice Architecture Biennale, 2012

defined by this tradition—a tradition of belief that "Virtue needs material possessions in order to appear dignified and beautiful."[1]

This belief led Renaissance patrons and architects to acknowledge that creating beautiful buildings and civic amenities is virtuous—and that mercantile trade is virtuous if it supports these works with finance. In fact, without orientation beyond profit towards virtuous expression in architecture, trade was considered dangerous—as wealth leads to the fear of losing it, and to sins that follow on from this fear. Civic Humanism is the rebirth of antique values that promoted the individual and the city they inhabited through the virtue of transforming wealth into beauty. Machiavelli and Erasmus called this the "exercise of virtue" and "organ of virtue". Alberti saw architecture as the professing of virtue, and one role of the architect was the teaching of virtue to patrons. Architecture manifests virtue he believed, re-presenting it as something civic.

Clare Guest describes the eloquent character of "Figural Cities", in terms of rhetoric and "the 'body' of civic virtue": "the civic virtues of Florence—its prudence, justice, magnificence—correspond to Aristotle's *Ethics*, but these virtues have become embodiments of the measure and harmony of virtue".[2] Guest suggests that the fifteenth-century Florentine writer Leonardo Bruni conceived of "the city as ornament", since ornament is a mode of virtuous contemplation. In making the connection between ethics and civic virtue, Guest reveals that ornament is an expression of "praxis, the essence and praise of civic life".[3]

In contrast to Florence, Claire Guest claims—citing Bruni again—"The *ornamenta* of other cities are instantly visible to a traveller, as an outer covering or shell... but anyone who goes... to the core or marrow (of Florence)" will find harmony between the buildings of a city, its parts, furnishings, paintings, streets: "the outer walls have not more ornament and magnificence than those within it, nor is one street or another handsome or beautifully kept and refined, but the parts of the whole city are thus".[4] Claire Guest indicates that Leonardo Bruni relates the 'magnificence of ceremony' to the excellence of Florentine festivals and this to its civic virtue—and ornament is thus revealed as a mode of ethos.

"The city is asserted as a totality", Guest claims, "but it is a totality asserted (almost imposed) by rhetoric, which insists on the architectural fabric as *ornamentum* in relation to its virtues.... Bruni's work shows quite clearly the rhetorical background to Alberti's efforts to articulate the union of the harmonious body of a building or the city, and the harmonious body of decorum; in each writer rhetorical ornament (*concininitas*) plays an important role. Fundamental to the union of physical fabric and 'body' of decorum is the understanding of justice as measure... as we should see Aristotle's discussion (in his *Ethics*) as essential to Alberti's view of proportion as ethical and mathematical.... As decorum requires that virtue has an outer form of corresponding splendour, so the visual aspect of the city places its virtues before the eyes, as in the funeral oration for Nano Strozzi, which celebrates the city through epideictic eloquence and 'the magnificent display of things'. The splendour of the city is not therefore a mere outer dress for the virtue of its inhabitants, but an excellence which penetrates through every part of the fabric of the city."[5]

---

1 Baron, Hans, *In Search of Florentine Civic Humanism: Essays on the Transition from Medieval to Modern Thought*, vol I, Princeton University Press, 1980, pp 236–237 (Baron is commenting upon and citing Alberti's texts *Vita Civile*, and *Della Famiglia*).
2 "Figural Cities", in *Rhetoric, Theatre and the Arts of Design: Essays Presented to Roy Eriksen*, ed Clare Guest, Oslo, 2008, p 158.
3 "Figural Cities", in *Rhetoric, Theatre and the Arts of Design*, p 166.
4 "Figural Cities", in *Rhetoric, Theatre and the Arts of Design*, p 160.
5 "Figural Cities", in *Rhetoric, Theatre and the Arts of Design*, p 160.

Opposite
David Grandorge, New Zealand House

Above
Civic Architecture exhibition, 2014, New London Architecture Gallery

Jan Bialostocki points out that Alberti's "second nature" was a "concept (that) enables him to consider architecture as an art of imitation", ie of nature: claiming that "Alberti then tries to establish which laws are being followed by nature as she strives towards perfection". Alberti places nature foremost as a model for representation and nature's laws as a guide for what is practical and ideal, calling this a "general law" of Congruity (*concininitas*). Alberti translates Aristotle's idea of mimesis into his proposition not only of nature as a guide to representation (decorum), but extends this to claim that nature is transformed by imagination and thus renews itself in the artist or architect's "perfection of nature". Bialostocki distinguishes this from the scholastic tradition, since "medieval writers always considered nature as a divine creation superior to human art", stating that "Human art could never, until the Renaissance, have been considered as surpassing nature."[6]

One other aspect of decorum is revealed in Bialostocki's attention to the Renaissance concern with "*Natura Naturans*". "*Natura Naturata*", is defined as "the imitation of created nature", a tradition which the Humanists inherited from the Greeks along with Ovid's emphasis upon "Metamorphosis". This was a tradition in which artists and farmers engaged together with what Petrarch called "cultivation". Cultivation of the natural world was seen in the Renaissance, as an example of divine will ("*Natura sive Deus*"). "For the Stoics", Bialostocki contends, "Nature was identical with life-giving power", something that was also revealed in imitation. Mimesis (as an act of cultivation) revealed man's cultivation, his participation with cosmic order. "*Natura Naturans*" is "a second concept, that of the imitation of creating nature". Alberti employs this second concept when he calls nature "marvellous artificer of things" and says, "nature itself seems to delight in painting".[7]

Alberti "formulated a new idea of great importance" Bialostocki claims—"Nature is perfect as a harmonious whole, but her elements are not"—enabling Humanists to see their task as the completion of, and perfection and participation with nature. From the Scholastic idea that man cannot surpass nature, that "art is infallible as nature" (*Grosseteste*), arose the idea that the "world is a living, animated, and intellectual being", (*Ficino*). Whilst for Alberti art begins with the imitation of nature, Bialostocki claims that for "Leonardo it is replaced by creation based on knowledge of necessity and inherent laws of nature". Bialostocki's argument is that whilst Alberti views nature as transformational—as a natural mode of mimesis—the innovations of Leonardo da Vinci and Mantegna ignore nature as transformation, seeing it instead as "perfect form". Bialostocki defines this as the beginning of "Mannerism" in art, whereby the history of art works became the model for artistic inspiration—not nature—"an order discovered by the searching mind and an analytical eye".[8] In other words, Historicist Formalism, ie architecture that refers only to it is own history, viewing this as something to be copied, like an *object d'art*.

Hans-Georg Gadamer insists that architecture cannot be thought of as an art work in this way, since one needs to "walk up to and experience a building in context". This involves imaginative participation, "In order for it to enrich our feelings for life." He is adamant also that in viewing art works as objects we misunderstand their vital role in the life of cities and their civic presence. He points out that 'even the freestanding sculpture on a pedestal is not really removed from the decorative context, but serves to heighten representationally a context of life with which it is decoratively consonant".

6 Bialostocki, Jan, "The Renaissance Concept of Nature and Antiquity", in *Renaissance and Mannerism: Studies in Western Art, Acts of the Twentieth International Congress of the History of Art*, vol II, Princeton University Press, pp 19–30.

7 Bialostocki, "The Renaissance Concept of Nature and Antiquity".

8 Bialostocki, "The Renaissance Concept of Nature and Antiquity".

David Grandorge, Victoria Street

DOMINE·JESU·REX·ET·REDEMPTOR
PER·SANGUINEM·TUUM·SALUA·NOS

Gadamer develops the context in which art works are viewed into a 'theory' of ornament and decoration based upon a view of decorum as lived experience. Gadamer's 'theory' saves art and architecture from the dead end of pointless aesthetics, "Art for arts sake", etc, and it does so by reminding us of their representational role;

> We have only to remember that the ornamental and decorative originally meant the beautiful as such. It is necessary to recover this ancient insight. Ornament or decoration is determined by its relation to what it decorates, to what carries it. It has no aesthetic import of its own that is thereafter limited by its relation to what it is decorating. Even Kant, who endorsed this opinion, admits in his famous judgment on tattooing that ornament is ornament only when it suits the wearer. It is part of taste not only to judge something to be beautiful *per se* but also to know where it belongs and where not.... Ornament is not primarily something by itself that is then applied to something else but belongs to the self-presentation of its wearer. Ornament too belongs to presentation. But presentation is an event of being; it is representation. An ornament, a decoration, a piece of sculpture set up in a chosen place are representative in the same sense that, say, the church where they are found is itself representative.... What we mean by 'representation' is, at any rate, universal significance of play. We saw that the ontological significance of representation lies in the fact that 'reproduction' is the original mode of being of the original art work itself.[9]

Gadamer sees the potency and relevance of architecture and sculpture to reside not only in site-specificity, but also in their consonance with location. He extends his argument to spatial settings to demonstrate that all of the arts are contingent upon witness, and as such, possess a potential public or civic character:

> Poetry and music, which have the freest mobility and can be read or performed anywhere, are not suited to any space whatever but one that is appropriate: a theatre, concert hall, or church. Here too it is not a question of subsequently finding an external setting for a work that is complete in itself but of obeying the space—creating personality of the work itself, which has to adapt to what is given as well as to create its own conditions (think only of the problem of acoustics, which is not only technical but architectural).[10]

This passage indicates that the recent tendencies of addressing architectural problems as subjective or aesthetic on the one hand, or as formalistic and pseudo-scientific on the other—or as we've become accustomed to, a confusion of both—obscures and represses the civic potential of architecture. Our work at Victoria addresses such potential indirectly, through the porous character of city spaces and facades, and directly, in the collaborative role that art, architecture and landscape play, as ornament and decoration, in articulating civic ecology.

---

9 Gadamer, Hans-Georg, *Truth and Method*, Sheed and Ward, 1960, p 159.
10 Gadamer, *Truth and Method*, p 157.

Opposite
David Grandorge, Westminster Cathedral, Victoria Street

Above
David Grandorge, Kingsgate House, Victoria Street (Burnet Tait & Partners 1966 demolished 2012)

10

Civic Depth

Peter Carl

VICTORIA PALACE
VICTORIA PALACE
Ring road (N)
West End
Ring road (S)
The City
Victoria Station

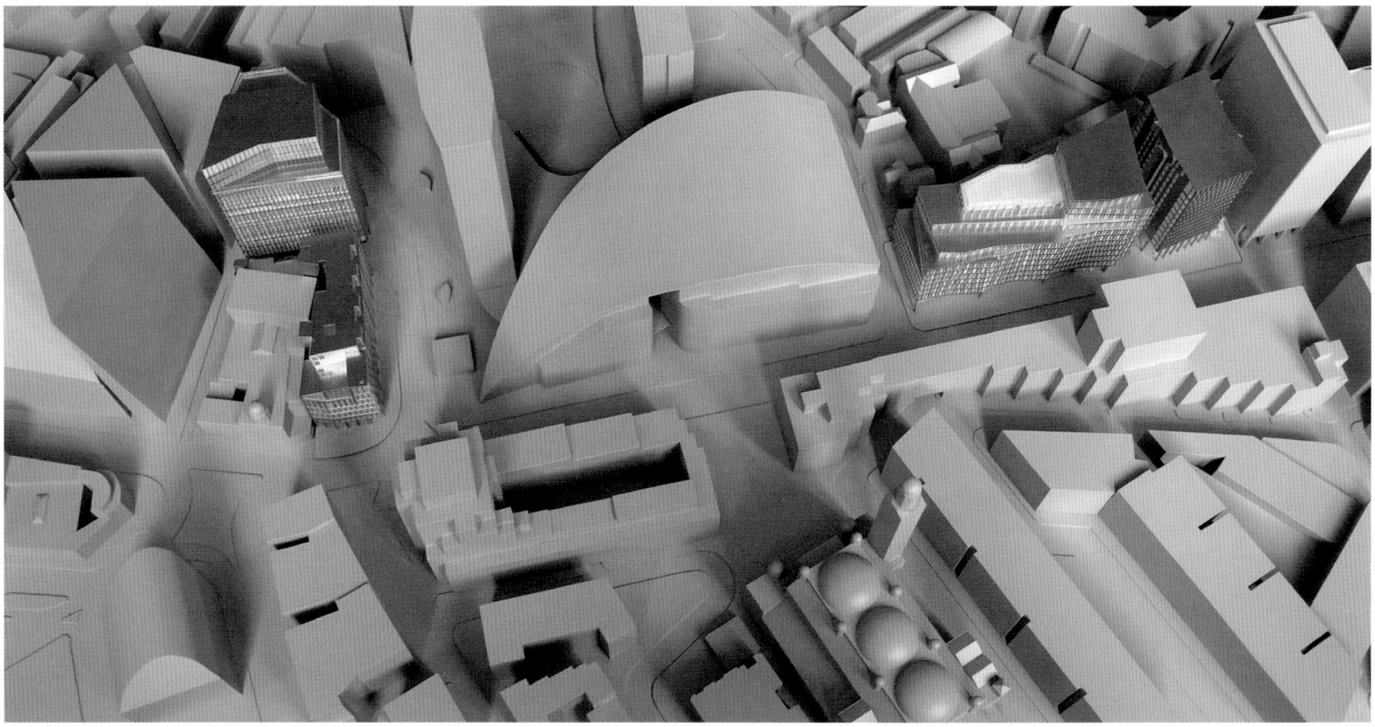

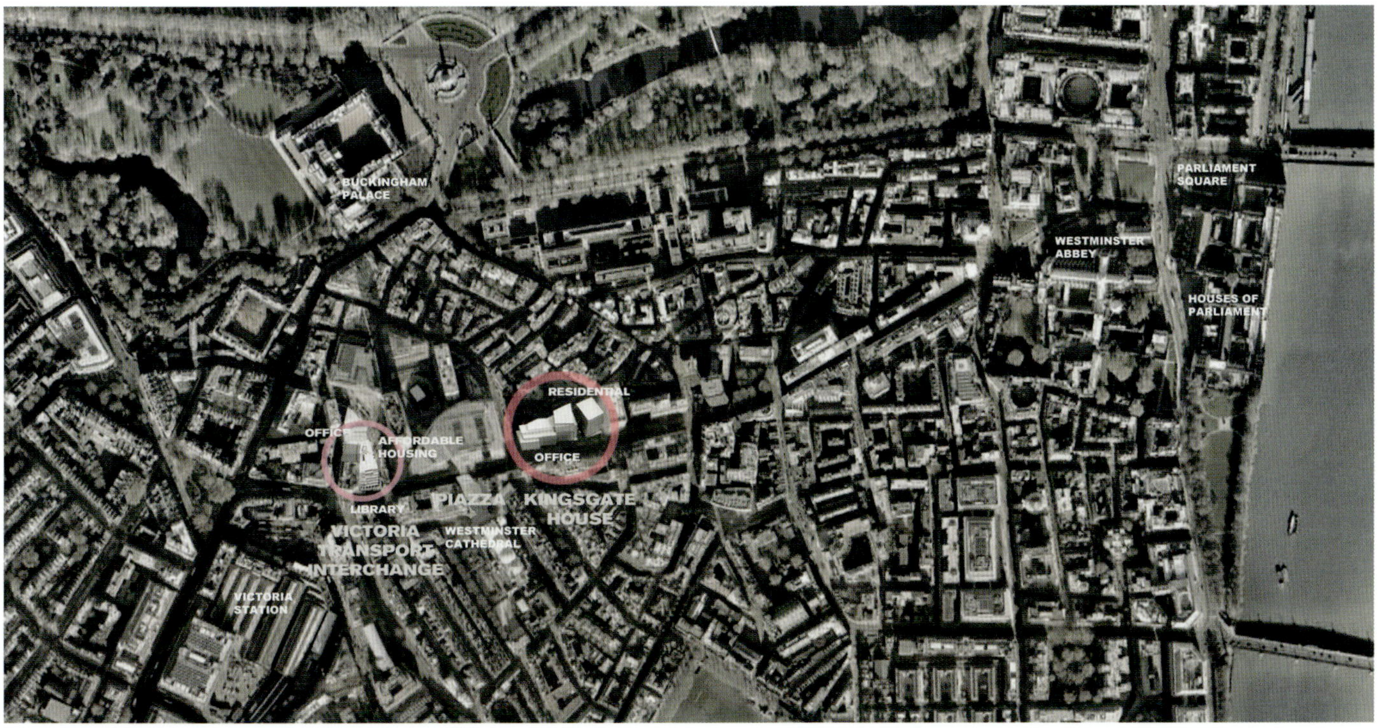

BUCKINGHAM PALACE
PARLIAMENT SQUARE
WESTMINSTER ABBEY
HOUSES OF PARLIAMENT
RESIDENTIAL
OFFICE
AFFORDABLE HOUSING
OFFICE
LIBRARY
PIAZZA
KINGSGATE HOUSE
VICTORIA TRANSPORT INTERCHANGE
WESTMINSTER CATHEDRAL
VICTORIA STATION

MUSES
Landscape
Figure
1 polyhymnia - choral poetry
2 Erato - lyric poetry
3 Calliope - epic poetry
4 Clio - history
5 Urania - astronomy
6 - Music?
7 - dance?
8 Thalia - Comedy?
9 Melpomene - Tragedy
Known
not yet fixed
celebration
Bodies

Everyone is generally in favour of 'Public Space', but it is not well understood. It tends to connote crowds going about their business or relaxing, very occasionally for protest (eg Occupy). These spaces comprise plateaux of granite, parks, streets, shopping malls, transport arrival halls (the last two often combined). Under these conditions, the public is seen as aggregates of individuals, exercising their freedom. To be sure, there is much of life that conforms to this vision of mass culture, mass consumerism, and so forth. However, the more this is the case, the more distant is this conception of public space from the political and ceremonial agora, forum or piazza, to which present-day 'public space' is often compared. We should distinguish between the crowd and the public, reserving 'public' for situations with political import.

It is common to oppose 'public' with 'private'; and the use of figure-field plans by architects and planners suggests that public is outdoors and private indoors. Accordingly, urban life is often wrongly understood to prevail between these two modalities. In fact, there is very little of a city that is purely private—perhaps the domestic loo. This is even truer of the cities of less developed countries. We should think in terms of a spectrum of public situations that penetrates the whole of urban life. Firstly, domestic affairs should not be thought as a refuge from urban conditions, but part of them. Beyond family politics (never simple), we meet our neighbours in living rooms, kitchens, doorways, yards and streets. At a next level of public meeting, we encounter friends, colleagues and new acquaintances at pubs or cafes, at clubs and associations and at places of work (which would range from hair-salon gossip through shop floors and offices to board rooms). At the most ceremonial level—therefore the most profound in terms of civic self-understanding, at least potentially—would fall law courts, parliaments and religious settings. When they are not simply flows of anonymous individuals commuting or shopping (lost in their mobile phones), crowds offer ephemeral moments of intensity—rallies, marches, sit-ins, riots and events like football matches or New Year's fireworks. However, it is the deeper institutional structure of public involvements that accounts for the persistent civic ethos. This ethos is not the wandering and relaxing under blue skies favoured in the renderings of 'public space' by architects and developers but proper involvements: conflict, negotiation, accommodation, collaboration.

It is therefore necessary to rethink 'public space' as a continuity of different settings; and rather than the bald distinction between private and public, we should think in terms of an urban depth. This is most obvious in the understanding of street, and in particular the High Street. Instead of thinking of it as a canyon between facades, filled with vehicles and crowds, we should imagine it as part of the institutional order of the city, as the seam between the depth of what lies behind the facades. This depth is marked by narrow streets and courtyards, which serve the diversity of lower-rent activities such as ateliers, clinics, educational establishments, libraries and archives, galleries, travel agents, eateries, speciality shops, churches, mosques, synagogues, dwellings, the semi-legal entities and so forth. These are also the settings whose architecture entertains happy and unhappy accidents, as well as material and spatial phenomena that tend toward gardens (there is more 'garden' in Paddington Station than in the lawn of the average housing-estate). On this depth-order a proper urban life depends, meaning a proper spectrum between social life, commercial affairs, political and legal debate and opportunities for reflection.

'Reflection' may seem to be a fragile or even elitist concern. Aristotle was the first and is still one of the few to ask what is the ultimate purpose of a city (not simply a place for transaction of goods and prevention of crime). He argues that a city grants the possibility of profound understanding of one's collective place in reality. The rites and ceremonies, which persisted until quite recently, accomplished the same thing, reconciling history with the cosmic conditions. Aristotle elevates this kind of insight, via tragic drama, to philosophical contemplation; but this is only the most articulate end of a spectrum that has its origins in the primordial spatiality of the civic topography.

Facade drawing of Victoria Street Library by Lynch Architects with iconographic drawings of sculptures of the 9 Muses by Hillary Koob-Sassen

This depth-order is, at present, virtually powerless against the monofunctional developments ("mixed-use" is generally a euphemism for shops) and their wind-blown plazas. The fuss about high-rise proliferation in London is less about the banality of translucent phalloi, an aesthetic problem, than it is about the loss of the depth-structure that gives proper place to, and therefore empowers, the manifold activities too easily generalised as SME's and affordable housing. Their inclusion in the spatial order of a city is a civic responsibility, for which there doesn't appear to be any institution capable of understanding, preserving or cultivating it, despite the advent of 'localism'. Accordingly, it is wholly commendable to see at Victoria Street this sort of understanding emerging from the initiative of Westminster Council, the developer Land Securities, the architect, Patrick Lynch, and beautifully captured in the photographs of David Grandorge.

The Victoria Street designs of Lynch Architects develop this depth both horizontally and vertically. Along the ground, the proposition establishes sequences of 'urban rooms' that penetrate the blocks and subtly adjust the decorum of public life from the crowd of the relatively neutral (and traffic dominated) Victoria Street to settings that acquire their character from the more differentiated block interiors. In this way such institutions as Westminster City School attain a presence upon Victoria Street. These mediating sequences are often oriented about garden metaphors, such as the forest photographs of Rut Blees-Luxemburg that appear as if engraved into concrete windows and develop analogies with shadows and an arcade. Particularly when illuminated at night, the setting suggests conditions propitious for the sort of urban chthonic reverie evoked in Max Klinger's etchings, *A Glove*, from late nineteenth-century Vienna.

Victoria Street Library sections through the staircase

Too often a simple by-product of systematic construction techniques, the rhythmic order of the edifices registers the movements of the sun both daily and seasonally (not only tempering solar gain but also providing conduits allowing the buildings to breathe). Rhythmic spatiality is, of course, one of the defining characteristics of architecture; but its meaning veers between the extremes of expediency and ritual. All aspects of ritual—speech, sound, movement and gesture, spatial articulation, ornament—are marked by rhythm, which in turn helps to situate the time-out-of-time of the rites within the deeper temporalities of origins and natural cycles. If we are no longer in the presence of rites at Victoria Street, and only the intimation of drama tragic or comic, there remains the fundamental reciprocity between volatile history and the primordial conditions to which we are also obliged. We encounter in Victoria Street a spectrum of social decorum which hides some of the darker shades of civic life evoked, for example, in Aragon's *Paris Peasant*; however, the attunement to metaphor in the design provides a context for reflection that is more profound than its neighbours' apparently more 'exciting' forms, hallucinatory glass and opulent capitalism.

Indeed Lynch Architects' scheme finds itself carving a properly civic order out of its more banal and noisy counterform. Not surprisingly, the nineteenth century topography—even including its transport and drainage networks—provides a more congenial reference to the full richness of a civic order than do the nominally imposing edifices more recently completed. The Lynch scheme's mediating sequences reach into the still-existing parts of the earlier topography in order to capture its analogical aspects, not for the sake of 'history' as such. As a result, the scheme is both more inclusive socially and also able to draw upon the earlier order's metaphoricity of earth in the extensive brick walls, the ornament and the light which pools within dark and hidden courtyards (in contrast to the uniformly glazed, maximum footfall 'transparency' favoured by capitalism's anxiety to secure returns by dressing itself in Scheerbart's expressionist crystal).

Consequently, and as against the neurotic futurism of its neighbours, the Lynch schemes supports a greater range of temporalities. This is particularly true of the western part of the street, and their two buildings that form part of the 'Nova' development, whose residences form a corner addressing Bressenden Place to the east; the grand undercroft of a new office building to the north; and, on Victoria Street, cradle a civic library adjacent to the existing Victoria Palace Theatre. The vertical topography of this library begins in the foyer with a stair

Victoria Street Library 1/50 scale bas relief sculptural models in travertine and alabaster by Hilary Koob-Sassen for the base and top of the staircase

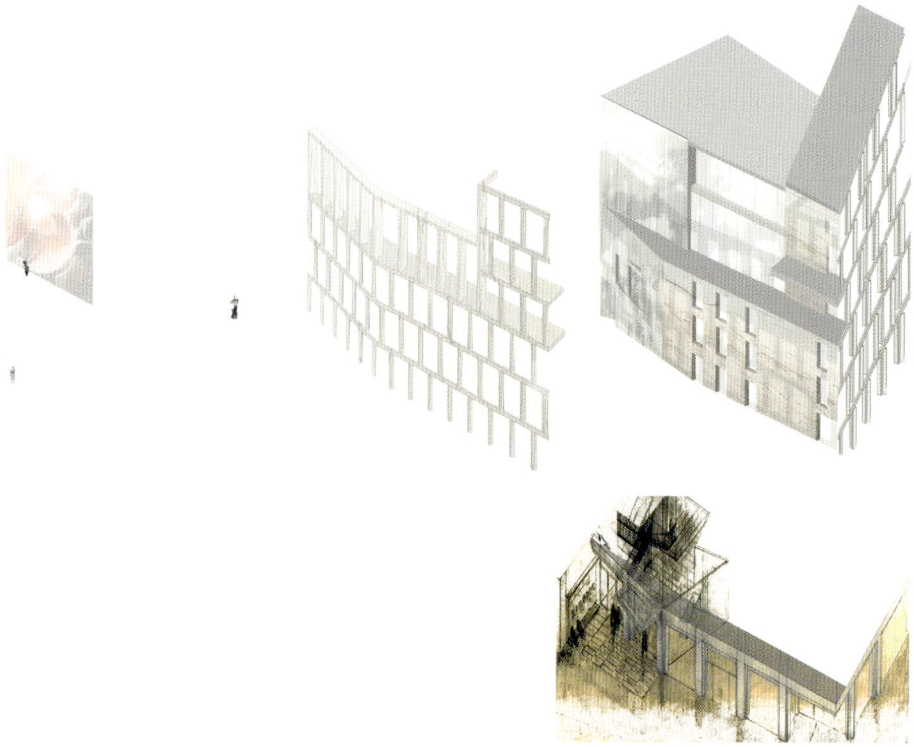

that doubles as amphitheatre-seating, complementing the chthonic reverie of the theatre next door and Victoria Station across the street with an explicit transformation of the glass wall into a *scenae frons* for actual performances. Hilary Koob-Sassen ornaments the ascent past the book stacks (memory) with bas relief sculpture that mediates between underground infrastructure and the theme of The Muses (knowledge, skill, the arts—diverse aspects of culture that are housed in a library). At the apex of the ascent one arrives at a species of celestial cave, suitable for use as a reading-room, dining room or civic meeting room. The room therefore embodies the discursive—social, political—and reflective possibilities of the scheme. Just as it receives the light in its dignified proportions and materiality and delivers it to the table, so reciprocally is the inhabitant granted views which summarise the civic horizon of London: to Victoria Station (southwest), to the River Thames (south), to Westminster Cathedral (southeast), to Buckingham Palace (north); to Westminster Abbey and the Houses of Parliament (east).

Above
Victoria Street Library exploded axonometric drawing showing the various layers of the south facade

Opposite
Victoria Street Library section south–north

1 Apartments
2 Public meeting room
3 Library cafe
4 Reading room
5 Library entrance
6 Victoria station ticket hall for Victoria line
7 Approximate location of District and Circle line

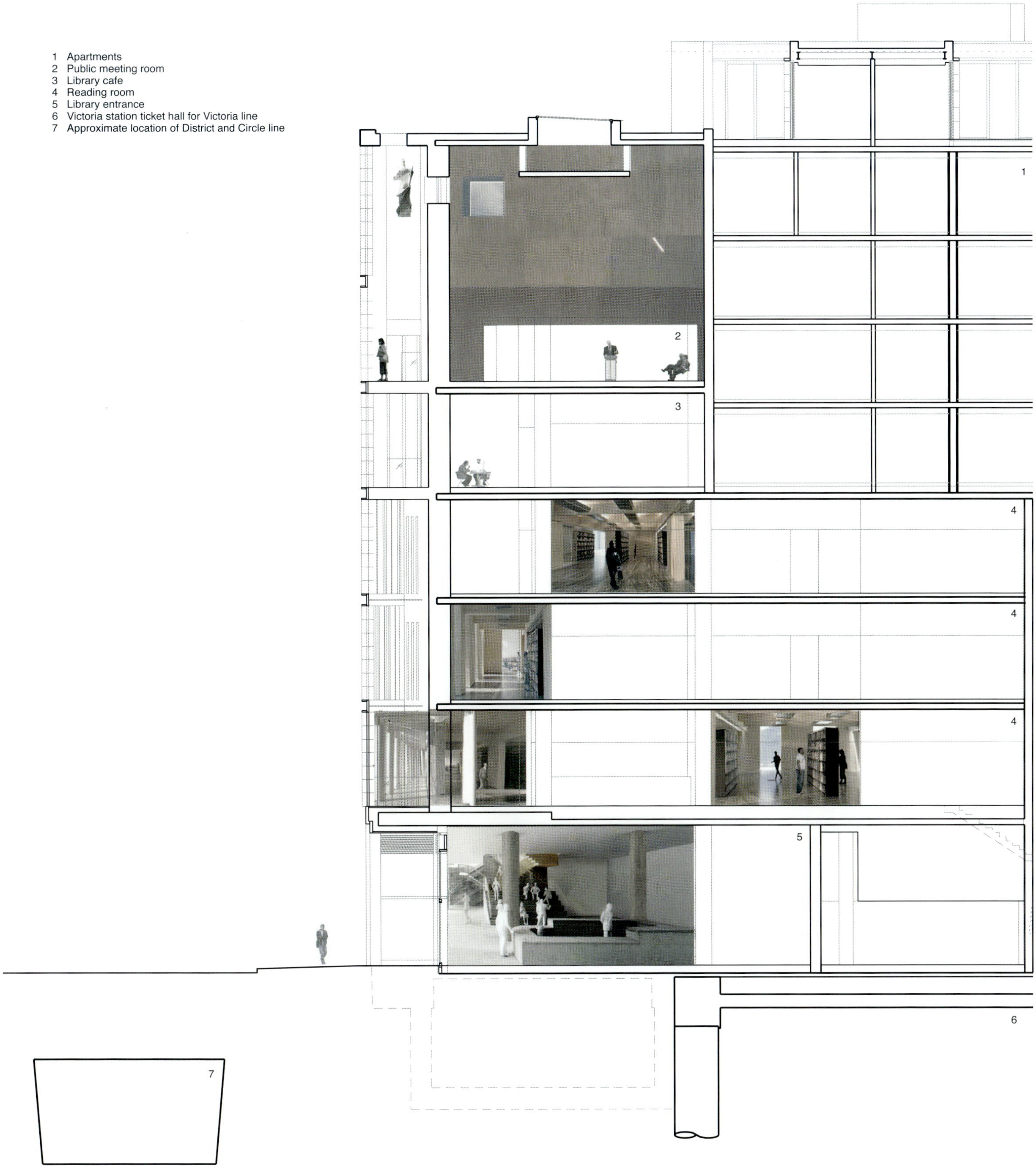

VICTORIA
PALACE
Purveyors of Celebrated Beers, Wines & Spirits
'BILLY ELLIOT REMAINS THE BEST SHOW IN TOWN'
'BEST MUSICAL OF THE DECADE'
VICTORIA PALACE

Above
Photographs of Inhabitable Models, Lynch Architects 1:3 scale model of Victoria Library, "Common Ground", Venice Architecture Biennale, 2012

Opposite
Collage showing southeast corner of Victoria library, housing and offices

VICTORIA
PALACE

VICTORIA
PALACE
VICTORIA LIBRARY

Opposite
Study collage of Victoria Street Library and housing with Nova East office building behind

Above
Sketches of housing courtyards sat behind Victoria Street Library

The Strange and the Familiar
Laura Evans

In 1894, the English architect John Francis Bentley was commissioned to design Westminster Cathedral, the Catholic cathedral in London. Subsequently, he embarked on a study trip that was to take in the great Byzantine churches of Europe; however, owing to an outbreak of cholera in Istanbul, he was unable to reach Hagia Sophia, widely regarded as the apotheosis of the era. Instead, stranded in Venice, he turned his attention to the city's cathedral, St Mark's Basilica, a collage of influences from across the Roman and Eastern worlds.[1] Shortly thereafter, he returned to London to begin work on Westminster Cathedral.

The result is a building which is like a dream of Venice, half-remembered upon waking; all bookmatched marble, mosaic, and even those distinctive coloured bottle-glass windows—famously seen at the Ca d'Oro. The Venetian influence extends beyond the architecture to the rituals of use; the famous celebration of Venice's marriage of the sea, *Lo Sposalizio*, is marked each year by the choristers of the cathedral.

The site for the new cathedral, formerly Tothill Fields Prison, sat just southeast of Victoria Street in the City of Westminster. Owing to the constraints of the surrounding area, when the cathedral was first built it was completely hemmed in by buildings on all sides, lacking the traditional piazza in front. Piazzas function not only as a setting for public life in the city, but also—in this context—as a place for ritual. For example, during the Easter Vigil, which takes place between sunset on Holy Saturday and sunrise on Easter Sunday, a fire is lit outside the church itself in order to light the Paschal candle, which is then processed through the darkened nave as the congregation in turn light their own candles from it. Symbolising the return of Christ, the rite bridges sacred and profane territory during the most important period of the Christian calendar.

In the early 1970s, two new office buildings—Ashdown House and BP House—were constructed to the north, opening up the cathedral to Victoria Street for the first time and making available a space which was re-appropriated as the piazza that the building had always lacked, arguably reinforcing the analogous relationship with St Mark's.

Bentley's Venetian journey was the starting point for our entry to an invited design competition for the redesign of Westminster Cathedral Piazza in the summer of 2010. Up until this point, the piazza had been a largely unconsidered space; flanked by the plant room grillage of the adjacent office buildings, scattered with bollards to prevent vehicular access and frequented by rough sleepers, it was utterly banal and entirely profane. The brief for the competition asked entrants to address these problems, and to reinforce the relationship between the space and the cathedral.

Our proposal placed Westminster Cathedral in the context of its influences, interpreting it—speculatively—as an ambiguous version of St Mark's. During the early stages of the design process, it was observed that there exists a coincidental relationship between the geometry of Piazza and Piazetta San Marco and that of Westminster Cathedral Piazza and Ambrosden Avenue. This is the point at which the design imagination comes into play; if Bentley's project can be considered to be the introduction of fragments of Venice to London, then this scheme aims to complete that, grounding the cathedral in an appropriate and useful public space, synthesising place and time, and making visible previously invisible relationships.

1 The 'collage' of St Mark's extends beyond mere stylistic and formal influences to the inclusion of literal *spolia*; physical fragments of older buildings brought back from military conquests. In fact, some of the *spolia* that can be seen at St Mark's were once part of Hagia Sophia.

Opposite
Study collage of Westminster Cathedral Piazza with proposed baldacchino

Top
David Grandorge, Westminster Cathedral Piazza

Bottom
Study collage showing the baldacchino of St Peter's at Rome juxtaposed with Westminster Cathedral Piazza shown during the inauguration of Westminster Cathedral in 1910

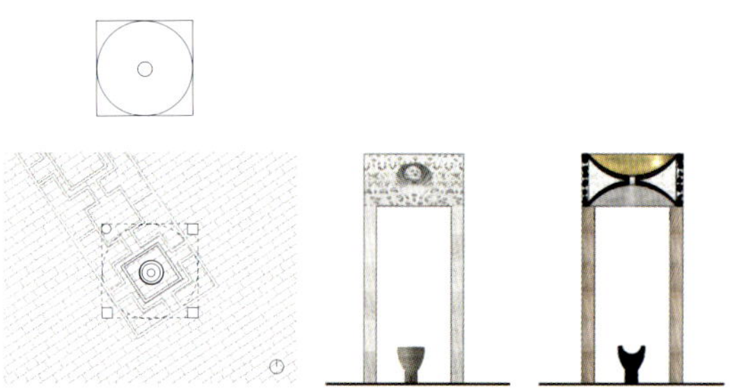

The Venetian relationship is reinforced by the introduction of inlaid marble setts in the same pattern as those found at the Piazza San Marco. Not merely decorative, this paving also delineates the territory of individual market stalls, allowing for a weekly food market to be established to serve the needs of local residents and further reinforcing the mundane use of the space.

Additionally, the scheme proposed to extend the sacred territory of the church by constructing a small, freestanding baptistery in the piazza. Taking the recognisable form of a baldacchino, the geometry of the new baptistery is derived from the proportions of the columns of the side aisles inside the cathedral, but, unlike the cathedral, it is oriented east–west. Used for adult baptisms and to light the Paschal candle, the font within would—for the majority of the year—be used as a drinking fountain for the homeless people who gather in the area to use the soup kitchen adjacent to the cathedral. The marble structure would be crowned with a filigrante frieze carved by a local sculptor, with tondos left blank at the centre of each of its four sides, awaiting images of new saints.

During the development of this project, the practice was simultaneously working on the early stages of another, far larger, project for Victoria Street, the redevelopment of Kingsgate House for Land Securities. Located on the north side of Victoria Street, adjacent to Westminster City Hall, the existing Kingsgate House was built in 1966 by Burnet, Tait and Partners. The existing building embodied all of the problems of Victoria Street; built in the 1860s as a major thoroughfare, by the middle of the twentieth century the construction of long, tall slab-blocks had rendered the street a traffic-choked canyon, cut-off from adjacent historic neighbourhoods to the north and south.

As with the Westminster Cathedral Piazza proposal, here too the initial design decisions arose from a speculative reading of situation and an imaginative leap. Diagnosing the problems of Victoria Street outlined above, we imagined a time where routes had connected the areas to the north and south of the street, and that our first move would be to reinstate these. The scale, proportion and geometry of these spaces would relate

Opposite
Ground plan showing geometrical relationships between Westminster Cathedral and Lynch Architects' proposals for the Cathedral Piazza with studies of the new baptistry/baldacchino

Top
Section and facade drawings of Westminster Cathedral Piazza with the new baldacchino

Bottom
Study collage showing Lynch Architects' proposals for Westminster Cathedral Piazza

to those existing elsewhere in the area; Westminster Cathedral Piazza, Cardinal Place, and Wilcox Place, making them feel as though they have always been there. Beginning with the ground of the city in this way, the buildings became secondary, allowing the proposal to operate as a critique of contemporary object-driven architecture.

Additionally, it was proposed to extend the development site to take in the lid of the cut-and-cover District and Circle underground railway line to the north. In collaboration with Vogt Landscape Architects, we designed a public garden which evokes a dried-up riverbed, a reference to the historic proximity of the site to the high tide mark of the River Thames prior to the construction of the Albert Embankment.

Through making many, many iterations of cardboard models, hand sketches, digital collages and simple CAD drawings, the orientation, massing, structure and appearance of two new buildings, one office and one residential, gradually emerged. This working methodology allows preconceived notions of how the architecture should appear to fall away, opening the process to chance and allowing unconscious influences to come to the surface. The introduction of serendipity into the activity of design is, we believe, a conduit which allows for mimesis to occur.

Considerations of orientation were of primary importance to the development of both buildings. Their southerly aspect onto busy Victoria Street necessitated the creation of layered facades which shield the occupants from both hot sunlight and the noise from the street below. We consider that these problems are not dissimilar to those faced by Giovanni and Bartolomeo Bon, the architects of the Ca d'Oro, a palazzo on Venice's major thoroughfare, the Grand Canal. The architectural approach there is similar; a grand, layered stone facade with recessed balconies protecting a domestic interior.

The residential building has a Jura limestone facade, with deep balconies sitting behind a stone screen that provides the residents with opportunities for privacy and also for appearance, the quintessential desires and poises of urban life. This stone exoskeleton also serves to partly conceal the varying window arrangements of the many apartment types contained within the building.

Study collages showing Westminster Cathedral Piazza and the new baldacchino in use during the Easter Vigil and on a spring morning

The office building has bronze-coloured extruded aluminium mullions which both protect from the sun and visually break up the mass of the building. The spacing of these fins diminishes on every successive floor, making the building appear taller and more statuesque than its bulk would seem to allow. Full-height solid ventilation panels—included to make possible rapid smoke purgation in the aftermath of a fire—open behind balustrades to form juliet balconies which allow for the partial natural ventilation of the offices within. At high level, secondary laminated glass pelmets with a printed onyx interlayer keep high summer sun at bay, and appear like glowing pieces of stone from within during the day, and from the street below at night. Roof terraces planted with Acers, a type of maple tree whose leaves vividly change colour throughout the seasons, provide outdoor space with views to the Houses of Parliament and to the river beyond.

Back at ground level, the courtyard we have created between the two buildings is flanked by bars and restaurants with an abundance of outdoor seating, giving life throughout the day and night to a place which—up until now—has been deserted from the moment that the crowd of commuting office workers flowed down the street to Victoria Station. Another, quieter, space is created between the residential building and Westminster City Hall, adjacent to the residents' entrance to the apartments. Here, a row of trees make a deep threshold between the entrance and the street, and the newly exposed flank wall of Westminster City Hall becomes the setting for a public art work by photographer Rut Blees-Luxemburg. *The Silver Forest*, drawing on sources such as Paulo Uccello's *Hunt in the Forest*, depicts numerous single-point perspective forest scenes cast into concrete panels flanked by pilasters. Seen from the residential entrance, nature and artifice appear to coalesce.

Some three hundred metres to the west, towards the station, another project to recuperate this part of London will soon emerge from what is currently a chaotic site, criss-crossed by sewers, railway tunnels, and other pieces of infrastructure associated with the ongoing station upgrade works. Here, as part of the Section 106 agreement for the Nova development site, Lynch Architects have designed a new library for Westminster City Council. The scheme, which also includes affordable and market housing and a new office building, is due to start on site in 2016.

Left
Study collage showing Westminster Cathedral Piazza in use for a summer wedding with Lynch Architects' proposed baldacchino

Right
Photograph of 1/20 scale plaster cast model with carvings by Hilary Koob-Sassen

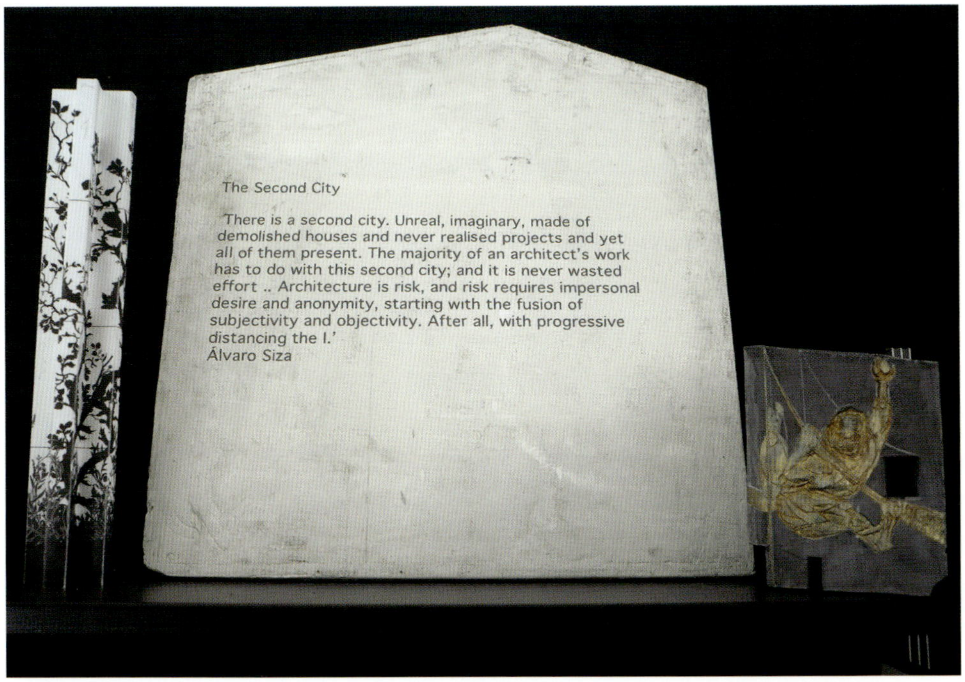

Nova East, a stand alone office building, is located to the north of the site, directly across Bressenden Place from Portland House, a 1960s tower block designed by Howard Fairburn and Partners, and due to be refurbished and converted into residential accommodation by David Chipperfield Architects. This is the area of the site in which the underground assets give rise to the greatest number of constraints; there are very few locations where the structure can be brought to the ground and, additionally, there is a requirement for access to the King's Scholars Pond Sewer—through which the Tyburn river now flows—at this point. A large steel truss carries the load of our proposed new office building, and this is encased in concrete to create a grand 'undercroft' at ground level, nine metres above the ground at its highest point. A vaulted concrete soffit clad with mirrored stainless steel evokes a reflective grotto, with circular apertures scooped out to mark entrances—and to give the required height above the sewer access zone for a mobile crane to operate when required. The edge of this undercroft space is demarcated by two enormous columns which carry the load of the building above. One of these, at the uppermost level of the terraced colonnade, hosts a drinking fountain; this also supplies water to enable a flower seller to set up a stall close by. A ground floor cafe sits at the lowest point of the sloping site, with tables and chairs placed outside in the summer months. The colonnade frames significant views from Cardinal Place, reinforcing this segment of an enticing, quiet pedestrian passage which will link Victoria Square in the west to Christchurch Gardens in the east, bringing into play Medieval alleys such as Seaforth Place, and previously static modernist spaces like Wilcox Place.

Back on Victoria Street itself, another building—Nova Place—wraps around the existing Grade II* listed Victoria Palace Theatre and the Duke of York pub. This mixed-use building contains a library on the prominent corner of Victoria Street and Bressenden Place, residential accommodation to the north, and a small office building on Allington Street. Taking as a model Renaissance palazzi—whose singular masses contain a multiplicity of functions—the disparate uses of this building are unified by a shared materiality; as at Kings Gate, Jura limestone and pre-cast concrete are used to form the facades throughout. This in turn reinforces the relationship of the building—and the

Opposite and above
Sketches and photographs of models of Victoria Street Library in Lynch Architects' studio

library in particular—to its civic neighbours, Victoria railway station and the adjacent theatre, creating a 'stone room' at the west end of Victoria Street, reminiscent of that at the east, Parliament Square.

As it forms the immediate setting of the listed theatre, the library facade has a great deal of significance both in civic and urbanistic terms. A skeletal outermost layer of solid Jura cruciform columns and beams protects a perforate stone wall behind, shielding the reading rooms within from excessive southerly sunlight. Taking a cue from its neighbour, Frank Matcham's Victoria 'Palace' Theatre, this limestone frame is also intended to provide a setting for sculptures, befitting a grand public building on a prominent London site such as this.

Within the library, glimpsed from the street, a large stair which doubles as an amphitheatre for children's storytelling connects the entrance directly to the reading rooms above. At the top of the building, with views to the south over the railway tracks winding their way into the station and the river beyond, sits a cafe, an external terrace and a double-height

toplit public meeting room, where public council functions such as planning committee meetings, as well as events associated with the town hall such as weddings and other ceremonies, would be held. This floor is also served by a separate stair and entrance from Victoria Street so that in the evening, when the library is closed, people can enjoy a pre-theatre meal in the cafe or attend a late event in the meeting room.

The architecture of these two spaces in particular—the stair and the meeting room—has been interrogated in countless large-scale physical models and collages throughout the design of the project. The working methodology of the practice consciously oscillates between the scale of a room and the scale of the city; what is it like to see a building from a significant place? What is it like to walk past it along the street? What do you see when you pass through the front door? How does it feel to be inside it? What is it made from? What can you see when you look out through a window, back across the city you have just left outside? Making models and collages of our buildings and the spaces within them ensures that questions like these, questions of city and of inhabitation, are constantly at the forefront of our minds, and prominent in the physiognomy of our buildings.

Above and opposite
Study collages, models and sketches of Nova East and Nova Place

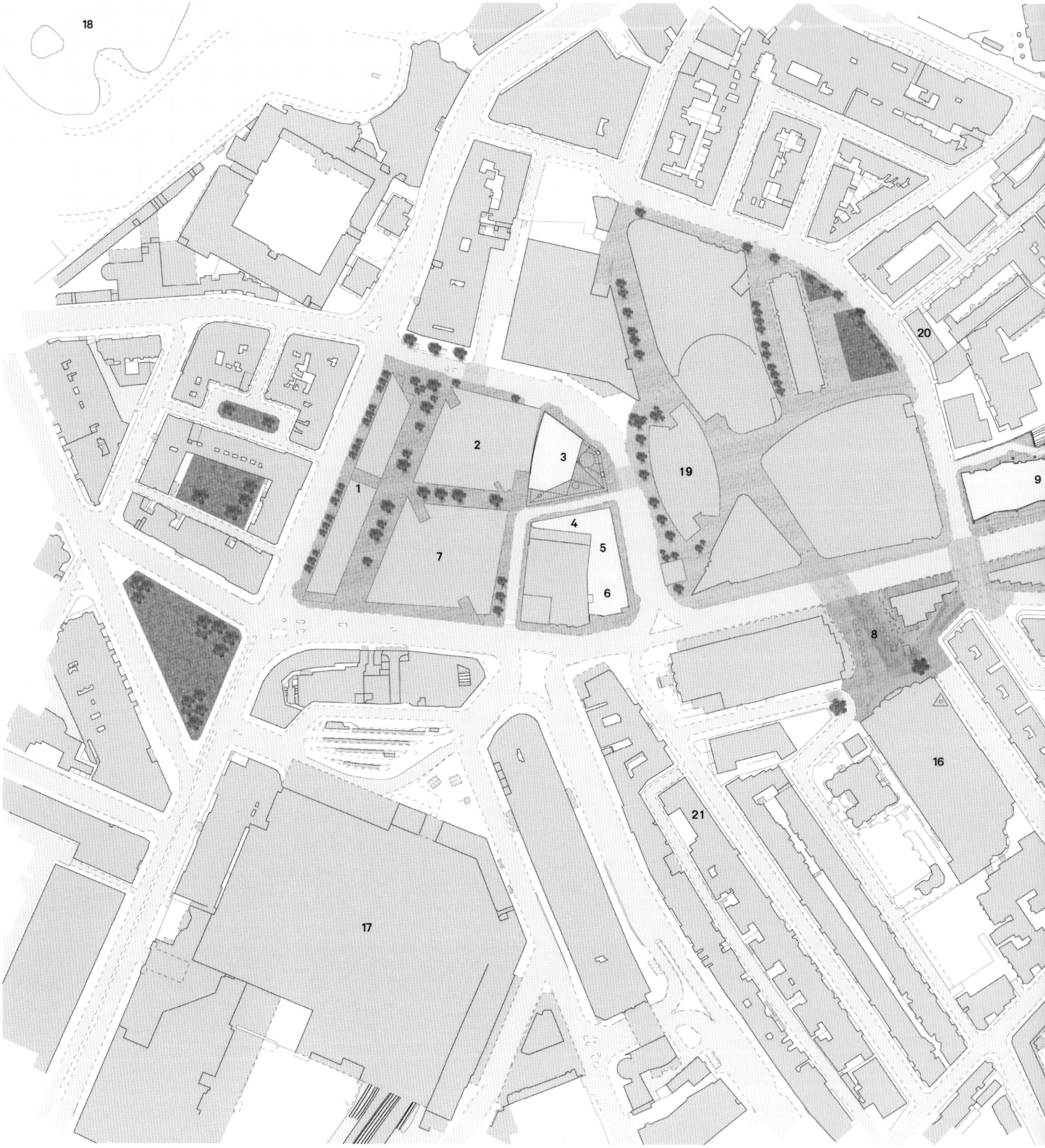
18
20
2
3
19
9
1
4
5
7
6
8
16
21
17

1 Residential building by Benson and Forsyth
2 Office building by PLP
3 Office building by Lynch Architects
4 Offices by Lynch Architects
5 Apartments by Lynch Architects
6 Library by Lynch Architects
7 Office building by PLP
8 Westminster Cathedral Piazza by Lynch Architects
9 Office building by Lynch Architects
10 Public spaces by Lynch Architects and Vogt Landscape architects
11 Residential building by Lynch Architects
12 Westminster City Hall
13 Westminster City School Extension by Lynch Architects
14 St James Court Hotel
15 Wilcox Place
16 Westminster Cathedral
17 Victoria Train Station
18 Buckingham Palace Gardens
19 Portland House conversion by David Chipperfield
20 Castle Lane conversion by Henley Halebrown Rorrison
21 The Passage by Buckley Gray Yeoman

Site plan showing the Land Securities projects on Victoria Street and the pedestrian public spaces linking Belgravia to the west (left) with Christ Church Gardens and Parliament to the east (right)

The Victoria Street work is a manifestation of both an attitude to the city and a form of practice which have been fine tuned within the office in recent years. Architectural, technical and structural problems, such as the need to purge an office floor of smoke in the event of a fire, or that to protect and access a sewer below ground, become opportunities for the exercise of civic and humane design, giving rise to, in the case of the former, a rare commercial building which can be naturally ventilated and, in the latter, a strange and intriguing space in the city, grand and generously proportioned, a gateway between developments previously conceived as if islands unto themselves.

As with Bentley's cathedral, our buildings seem to me both deeply familiar yet ineffably strange; the result of close study both of the past and of present problems, and the application of what might be called the "design imagination" to both. In his 1919 essay, "Tradition and the Individual Talent", TS Eliot speaks of something he terms "the historical sense" in writing, saying "... the historical sense involves a perception, not only of the pastness of the past, but of its presence; the historical sense compels a man to write not merely with his own generation in his bones, but with a feeling that the whole of the literature of Europe from Homer and within it the whole of the literature of his own country has a simultaneous existence and composes a simultaneous order. This historical sense, which is a sense of the timeless as well as of the temporal and of the timeless and of the temporal together, is what makes a writer traditional. And it is at the same time what makes a writer most acutely conscious of his place in time, of his own contemporaneity."[2] This simultaneity of past and present, real and imagined, and strange and familiar gives rise to recognition and delight in architecture, and it is these qualities that we hope our work brings to a part of London from which they have been conspicuously absent since Bentley sailed back from Venice over one hundred years ago.

---

2 Eliot, TS, "Tradition and the Individual Talent" in *The Sacred Wood*, New York: Alfred A Knopf, 1921, p 44.

Above
Photograph inside The Zig Zag Building and material studies for The Zig Zag Building and Kings Gate

Right
Study of the geometrical spatial characters of the public spaces on Victoria Street and in-between The Zig Zag Building and Kings Gate

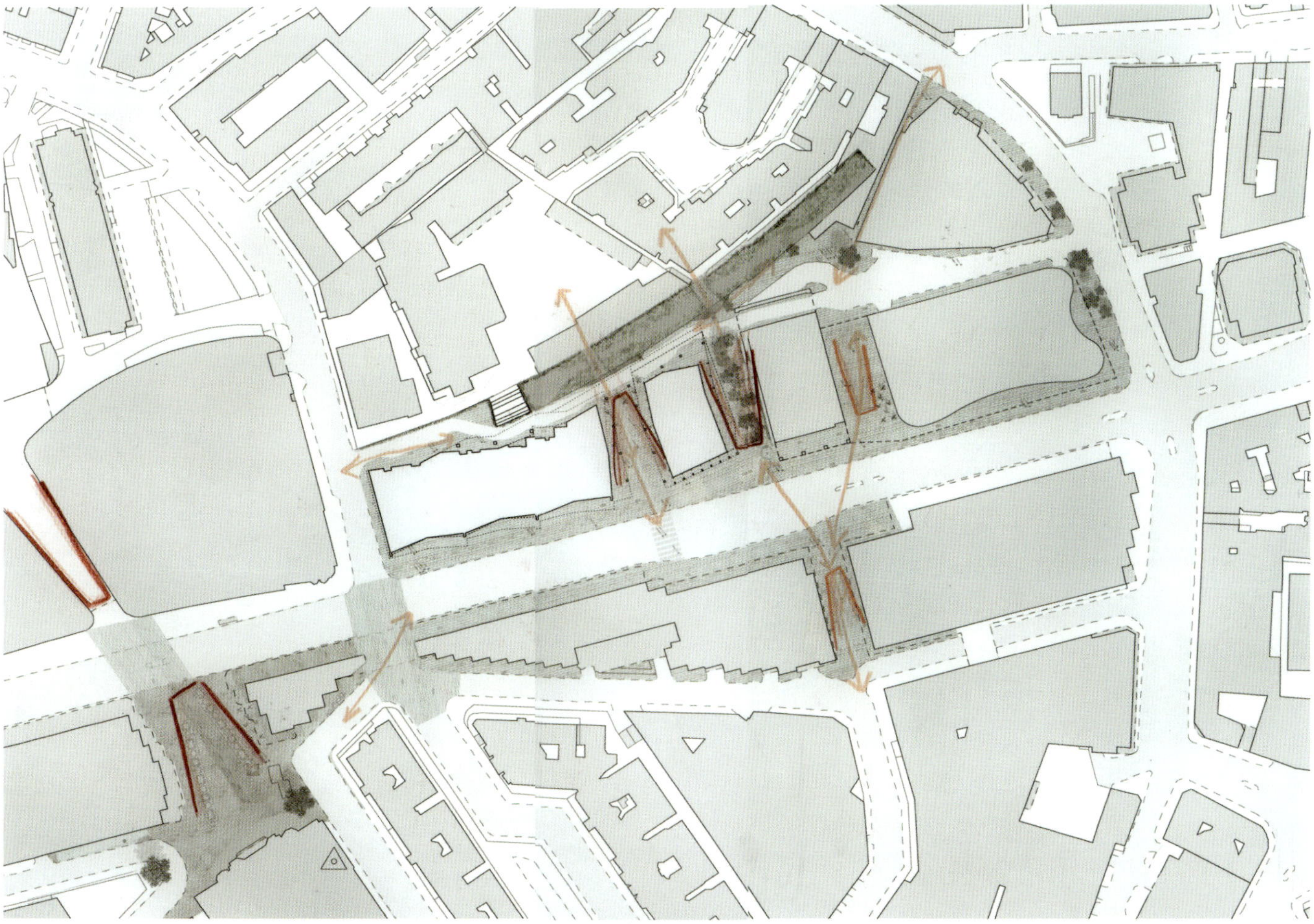

V Λ

RENEWING THE CITY
RENOVATIO URBIS
VICTORIA STREET SPACES
GENIUS LOCI

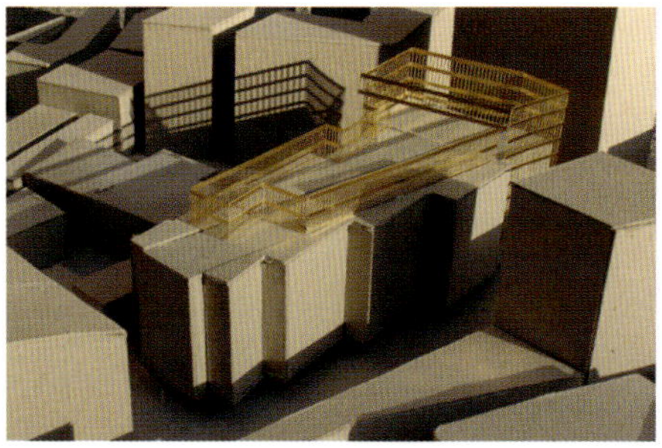

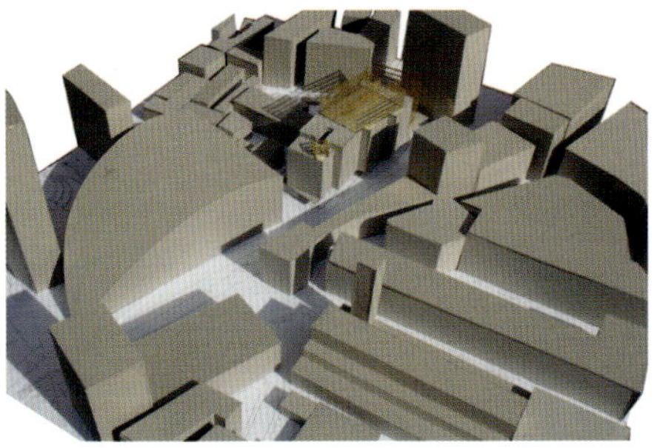

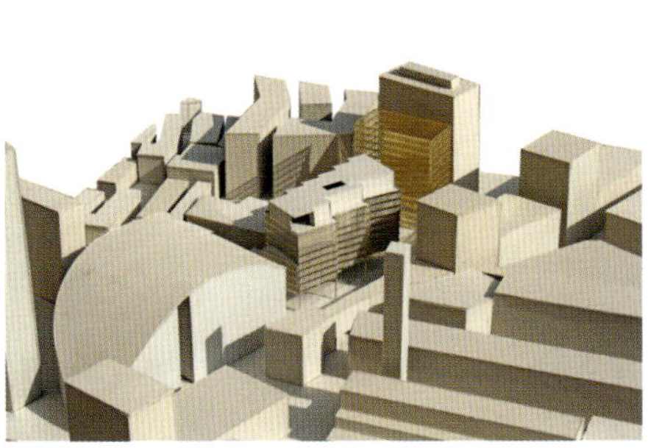
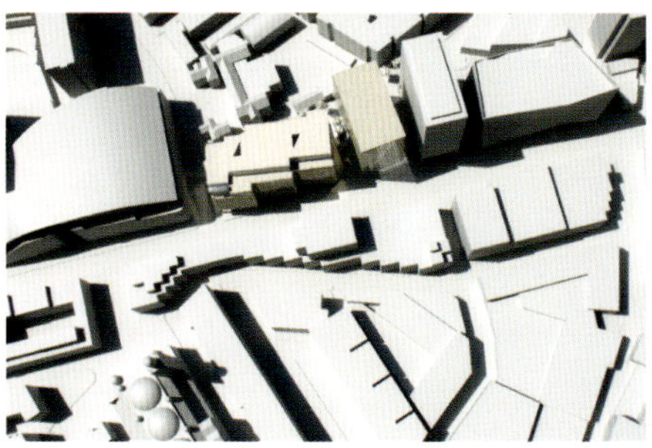
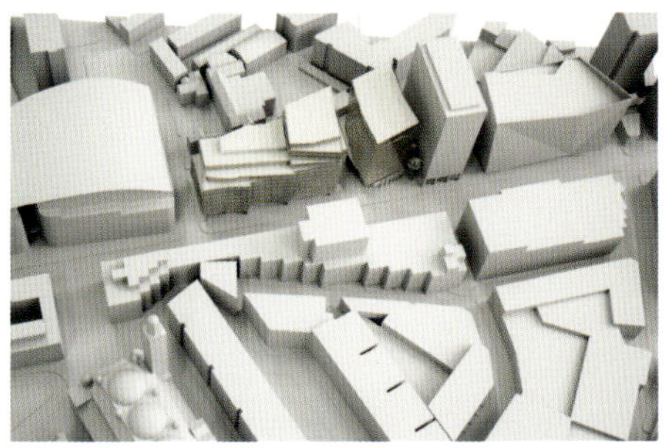

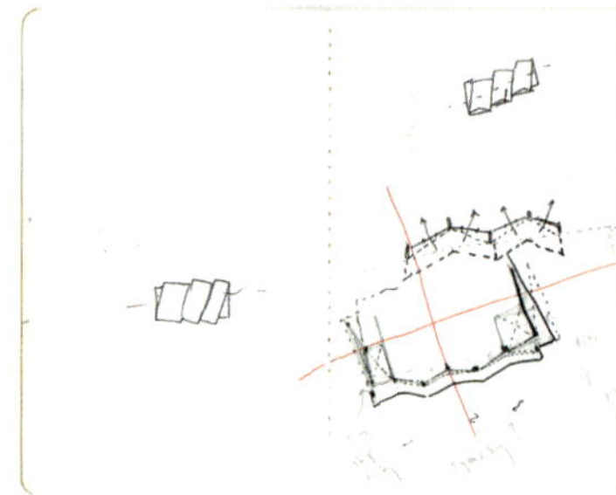

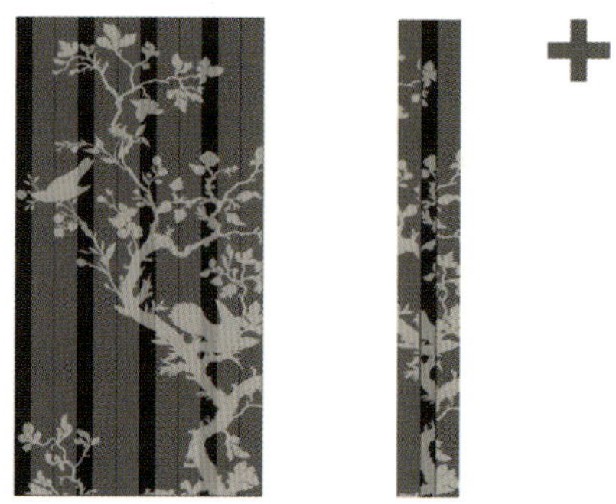

Drawings, model photograph and studies of The Zig Zag Building and drawing by Timoraus Beasties of the "Birdstane" column for Kings Gate

Model photograph and studies of Kings Gate

westminster cathedral
portland house
victoria library
victoria line tube station
vincent square
victoria line
cardinal place

Patrick Lynch, Study of Victoria Street and Westminster showing a network of civic institutions as urban rooms

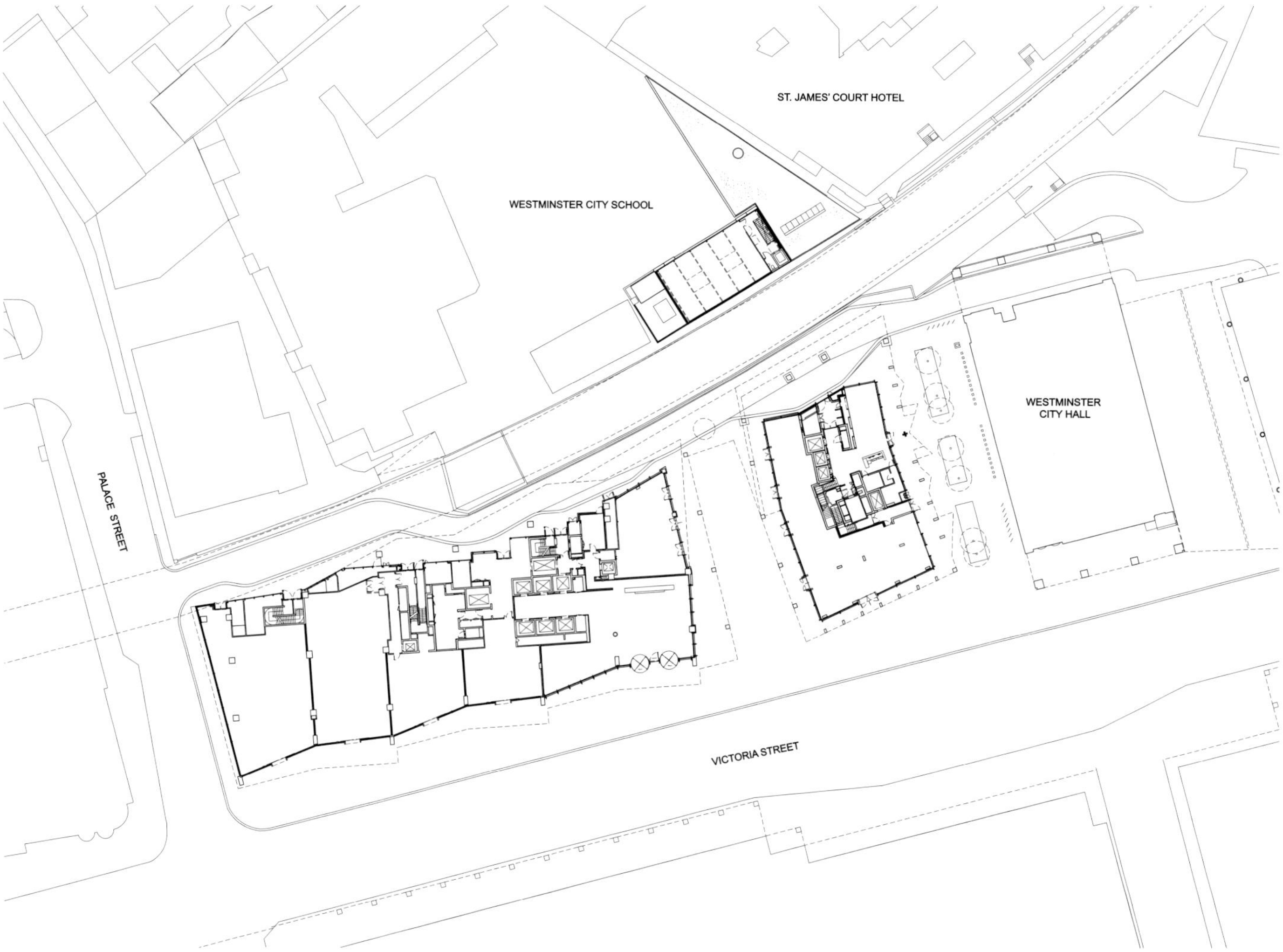

Site plan showing ground floor plans of The Zig Zag Building and Kings Gate

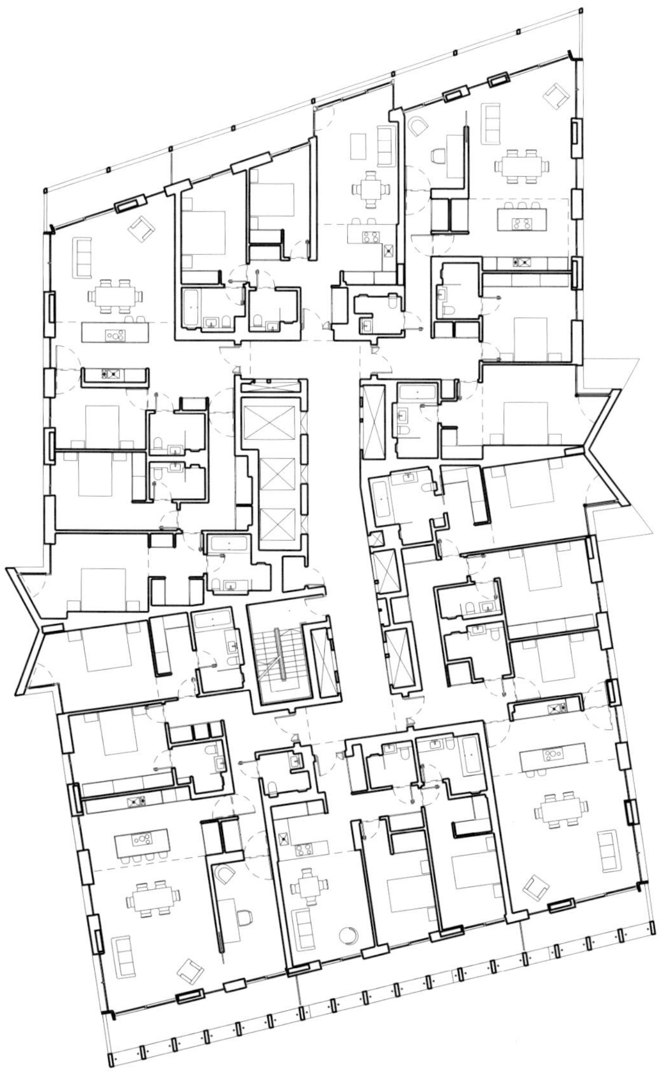

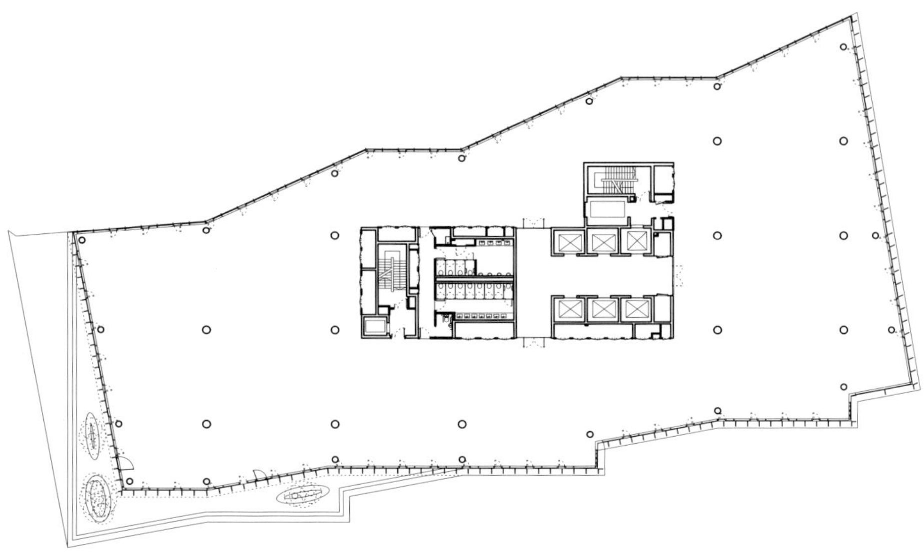

Top
Typical upper floor plan (levels 8–11) of Kings Gate

Bottom
Typical upper floor plan (level 8) of The Zig Zag building

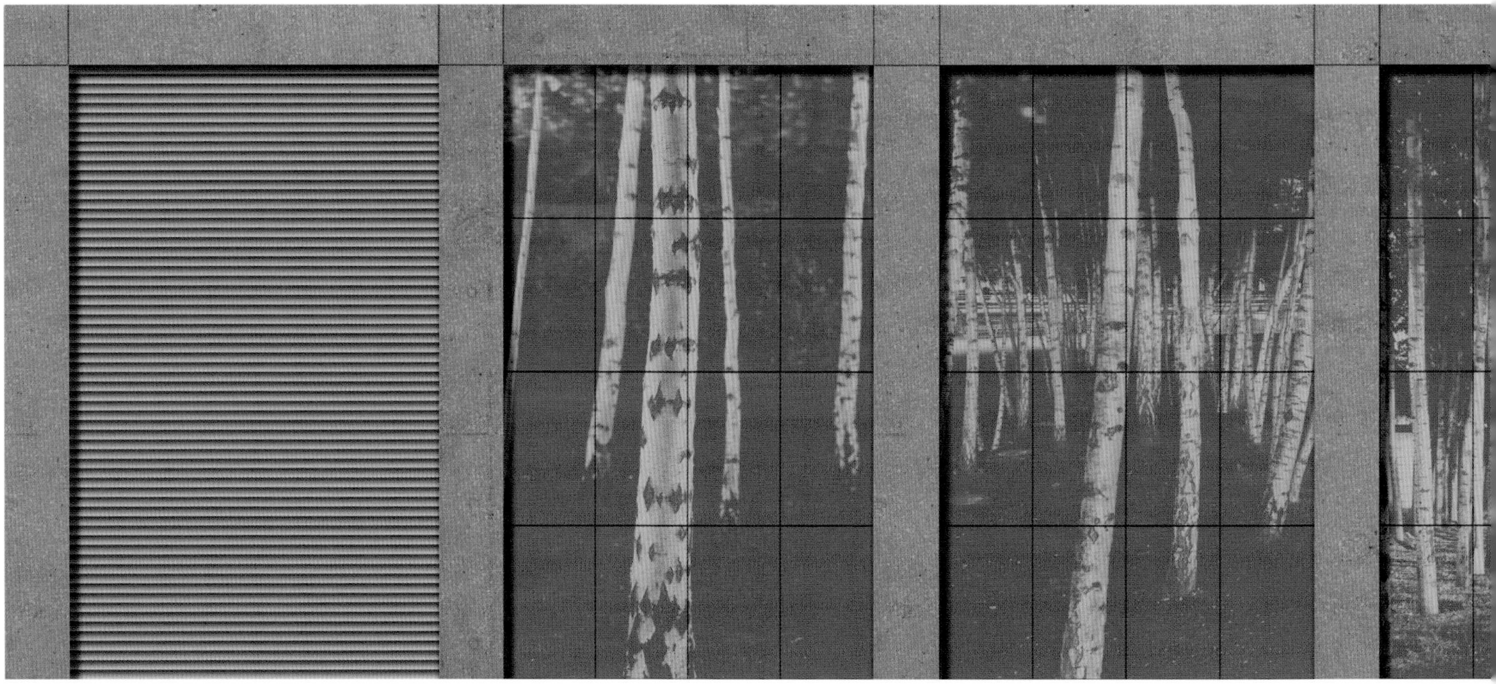

Elevation drawing showing *The Silver Forest* art work by Rut Blees-Luxemburg on the western facade at ground level of Westminster City Hall, approx 8 x 30 m

JAMIE
OLIVER
WESTMINSTER CITY HALL

CITY HALL
64

ITALIAN
WINE

WESTMINSTER
CITY HALL

WESTMINSTER
CITY HALL

ZERO TOLERANCE
for

STAFFORD PLACE SW1

A

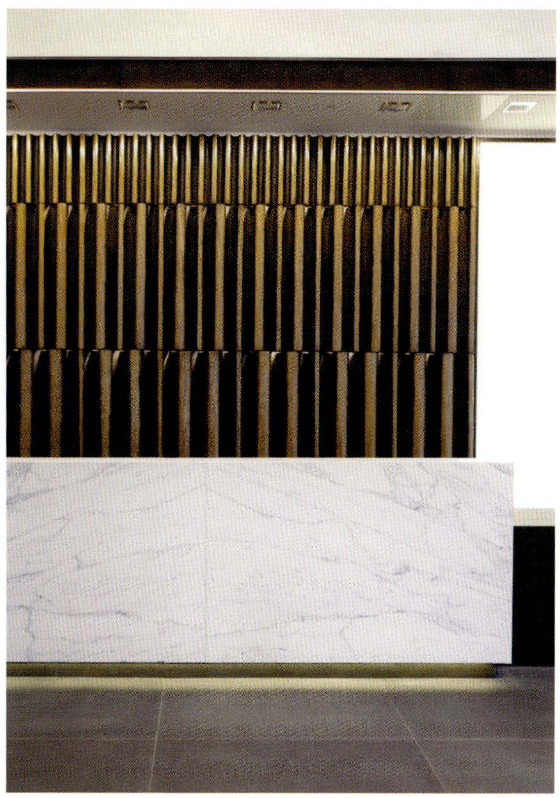

Mimesis and Imagination
Patrick Lynch

Design seems to involve as much looking as thinking, and as much remembering as imagining. In this way, it is not dissimilar to a first encounter with a new building or a strange place—where orientation is dependent upon interpretation of experiences of typical situations, and unconscious anticipation of what will happen next. Similarly, reading someone's impressions of a building that you have designed is an odd experience for an architect—both uncanny and strangely familiar. It has more in common with a dream than anything else. If you are an architect who is also a writer—and arguably we all are to some degree—you are used to a certain disjunction between images, metaphors and physical experiences. Yet, encountering architectural criticism is a physical and psychic shock, unnerving: like seeing something unexpected suddenly and fleetingly reflected in a mirror. Despite your own conscious recollection of a catalogue of memories and half remembered images and atmospheres, critics sometimes recognise references to buildings and places that you had forgotten, or weren't even aware that you knew about. In most cases, their references are not yours at all, and if you allow it, an architectural project can have the unexpected effect of beginning conversations about the power of memories, the role of archetypes, and the significance of cultural differences. Writing about our Victoria library project in 2014 Flora Samuel claimed that "Spatial games and historical quotations are clearly present in this highly intellectual composition, evidently an immense investment of care on the part of the architect. This gives the library the necessary authority for this august location. It won't be outdated in a hurry."[1] This is, of course, exactly the sort of critique that any literate architect would wish for, but its also unnerving. She continues, "Kings Gate has a layered facade that fits immaculately well into its surroundings, offering colonnaded urban space at base level. I can actually read the layers of architectural history that have gone into its evolution." What layers can she read in the drawings and images of the buildings? And how can one's memories of buildings and situations communicate themselves so readily?

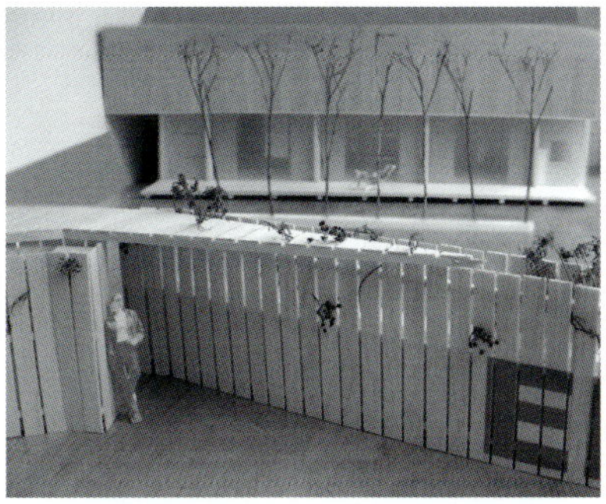

It is curious that a new building can immediately orient you somewhere. Buildings seem to contain—all at once—recognition, surprise, memory, expectation, premonition and anticipation. In Baroque architecture for example, the tension between 'deformation' and 'reformation' creates rhythmic, geometric and atmospheric richness—vitality and excitement—as you move across and through facades, staircases and courts. This theatricality depends upon a certain amount of recognition of a continuity of references, and disorientation is a vital aspect of the drama of spatial continuity, albeit a sensation that is dependent upon continuity as much as discontinuity.[2]

This essay, and the others in this book, are reflections on the phenomenon of mimesis in architecture, and concern more or less specifically its appearance in the work of my practice. I'm painfully aware of the differences between words and images and the reality of architectural experience—when I hear an architect speak about their work I can't help remembering the words of a critic: "Put your hands on the car, and step away from the metaphor", but I can't help remaining curious about the relationships between words and buildings.

Drawings and models allow you to get quite close to experiencing the qualities of spaces and allow you to adjust the proportions of things, but nonetheless there are things that you cannot understand as a designer as a sequence of images and memories and moods unfurl

Opposite
Patrick Lynch, Sketches of the new hall of the ELBWO Centre, London, E7

Above
Model photographs and photograph of the ELBWO Centre

Overleaf
Ground plan, section and street facade

1 *Blueprint*, 23 April 2014.

2 Lynch, Patrick, *The Theatricality of the Baroque City*, Dr Müller Verlag, 2011 (this originated in my MPhil dissertation at Cambridge University supervised by Dalibor Vesely, 1996). See also "Practical Poetics: Rhythmic Spatiality and the Communicative Movement between Site, Architecture and Sculpture", unpublished PhD dissertation, Patrick Lynch, The Cass, 2014 (supervised by Peter Carl, Helen Mallinson and Joseph Rykwert).

Photograph of the ELBWO Centre,
destroyed by arson, 2004

inside and before you. It is in this latent territory of imagination, neither entirely linguistic or typological, nor purely tectonic or spatial, that mimesis operates within architecture. In order to try to describe this territory, I will refer to some of the philosophical and artistic ideas that structure my work as an architect, and in particular to the tradition of hermeneutics.

In *Mimesis: The Representation of Reality in Western Literature*, Frank Auerbach likens his approach to "those modern writers who prefer the exploitation of random everyday events, contained within a few hours and days, to the complete and chronological representation of a total exterior continuum… they hesitate to impose upon life, which is their subject, an order which it does not possess in itself".[3] He describes his method as "letting myself be guided by a few motifs which I have worked out gradually and without a specific purpose", and justifies this, "for there is always going on within us a process of formulation and interpretation whose subject matter is our own self. We are constantly trying to give meaning and order to our lives in the past, the present, and the future, to our surroundings, the world in which we live; with the result that our lives appear in our own conception as total entities—which to be sure are always changing, more or less radically, more or less rapidly, depending on the extent which we are obliged, inclined, and able to assimilate the onrush of new experience."[4] Auerbach defends modern mimesis in terms of its psychological and phenomenal realism: "These are the forms of order and interpretation which the modern writers… attempt to grasp in the random moment—not one order and one interpretation, but many, which may either be those of different persons or the same person at different times; so that overlapping, complementing, and contradiction yield something that we might call a synthesised cosmic view or at least a challenge to the reader's will to interpretative synthesis."[5] He notes the emergence of this view in the early twentieth century in contrast to the "pseudo-scientific, syncretistic and primitive" views of various "sects": "the temptation to entrust oneself to a sect which solved

---

3 Auerbach, Frank, *Mimesis: The Representation of Reality in Western Literature*, Princeton University Press, 1953, 2003, p 548.

4 Auerbach, *Mimesis: The Representation of Reality in Western Literature*, p 549.

5 Auerbach, *Mimesis: The Representation of Reality in Western Literature*.

Study drawing and model photograph of Lynch Architects' competition winning proposals for Barking Abbey Green

all problems with a single formula, whose power of suggestion imposed solidarity, and which ostracised everything which did not fit in and submit—this temptation was so great that, with many people, fascism hardly had to employ force when the time came for it to spread through the countries of old European culture, absorbing the smaller sects".[6] Mimesis, he suggests, implies a political dimension related to freedom and creativity both in art, and in life generally.

Dalibor Vesely, describes mimesis as "creative imitation in which something with the potential to exist is recognised and reenacted as a significant gesture; it may be sound, as song or music; visible reality, as image or picture; or ideas, as an articulated and structured experience" (ie architecture).[7] He claims that "we do not as a rule think about architecture as being a mimetic art", because 'this disinclination has partly to do with the well-established tradition in which architectural mimesis was reduced to imitation of reified precedents, such as the primitive hut, the Solomonic Temple, exemplary buildings, and so on, or to such generalised notions as 'the imitation of nature'."[8] Vesely believes, however, that architectural representation is closely related to mimesis as *decorum*. Decorum is a term in classical poetics and rhetoric that describes the appropriateness (*prepon*) of dramatic emphasis, and the relationships between content and expression. Crucially, in terms of mimesis, decorum is not in itself representation, but a quality or sensibility and judgement of poetic measure: "Mimesis is not the same as imitation; classical thinkers saw it as a particular form of *poiesis*."[9] Vesely's observation is based not only on Plato's insistence that 'every artist is a poet',[10] but also on Aristotle's description of art as "the imitation of praxis".[11] He defines praxis as "living and acting in

---

6 Auerbach, *Mimesis: The Representation of Reality in Western Literature*, p 550.

7 Vesely, Dalibor, *Architecture in the Age of Divided Representation: The Question of Creativity in the Shadow of Production*, MIT, 2004, p 287.

8 Vesely, *Architecture in the Age of Divided Representation*, p 366.

9 Vesely, *Architecture in the Age of Divided Representation.*

10 Vesely, *Architecture in the Age of Divided Representation*, Vesely cites Plato, *Symposium*, 204b-6.

11 Vesely, *Architecture in the Age of Divided Representation*, p 367, Vesely cites Aristotle: "It is mainly because a play is a representation (*mimesis*) of action (*praxis*) that it also for that reason represents people as doing something or experiencing something (*prattontes*)", *Poetics*, 1451b10.

accordance with ethical principles" and also as "people doing or experiencing something but also things that contribute to the fulfilment of human life".[12] One definition of poetics is "making", and as such "(*poiesis*) is the bringing into being in the world something that did not previously exist".[13] If mimesis plays a role in both praxis and poetics, this suggests that they are complimentary in a practical art such as architecture, if, albeit, often in tension. This tension arises from the directed nature of architectural work and from the mysterious character of mimesis, which hints at a deeper ambiguity in imaginative creativity arising from the interplay of intentionality and chance. Arguably, this tension is not only characteristic of our work as architects, which strives towards order of sorts, but also of the nature of order itself. Vesely notes that "mimesis reveals the mystery of order as a tension between its potential and actual existence".[14]

I think that "potential" describes the essential character of design energy, situated somewhere between knowledge and anticipation, direction and imagination. I believe that the mimetic potential of architecture resides in the ambiguity of our commissions and in an architect's creative resolution of practical and artistic problems. The directed nature of this work can be compared to the role that "plot" (*mythos*) plays in drama. On the one hand: "Each project, however small or unimportant, begins with a program—or at least with a vision of anticipated result. Such a program or vision is formed in the space of experience and knowledge available to each of us. The result can be seen as the single actualization of an infinite number of possibilities",[15] and on the other hand, architecture is not merely an example of "the science of poetics, known better as aesthetics",[16] but of the "poetic paradigm" (or "poetic mythos"), because, otherwise "how could architecture, painting, and practical life ever meet?"[17] Their capacity to meet lies in the mimetic potential of each new commission I believe—the potential for a project to become part of a whole. You might say that decorum is the *barometer* of the mimetic potential of architecture to articulate latent order. Which is why it is possible for us, Vesely claims, to "speak about poetic mythos as the soul of all the creative arts, including architecture".

There is a tension between the banal aspects of singular commissions and the artistic potential in design problems of course. This tension is implicit in praxis in general, Peter Carl claims, since "One always finds oneself in an agonic movement between particular and universal, between concrete many and symbolic one, between dialogue and dialectic... between earth (conditions) and world (possibilities), which points to the universal nature of 'situation' (all situations involve interpretation)."[18]

In other words, you might say that architecture is an exemplary mode of praxis, and an art, because it reconciles programme (plot, myth) and craft (technique, poetics) with specific situations; and it does so in relation to the broader context of typicality and order. Hans-Georg Gadamer claims in fact that:

> Testifying to order, mimesis seems as valid now as it was in the past, insofar as every work of art, even in our own increasingly standardised world of mass production, still testifies to that

12 Vesely, *Architecture in the Age of Divided Representation*, p 368.
13 Vesely, *Architecture in the Age of Divided Representation*, pp 12–13.
14 Vesely, *Architecture in the Age of Divided Representation*, p 288.
15 Vesely, *Architecture in the Age of Divided Representation*, p 13.
16 The passage cited is from an unpublished manuscript version of Vesely's *Architecture in the Age of Divided Representation: The Question of Creativity in the Shadow of Production.*
17 Unpublished manuscript version of Vesely's *Architecture in the Age of Divided Representation: The Question of Creativity in the Shadow of Production.*, p 368.
18 Carl, Peter, "Geometry and Discourse", unpublished essay, 2010.

Top
Photograph of Barking Abbey ruins in use for an orthodox mass and pilgrimage

Bottom
Photograph of Barking Abbey Green during consultation with local residents

> deep ordering energy that makes life what it is. The work of art provides a perfect example of that universal characteristic of human existence—the never-ending process of building a world.[19]

Why then, did Aristotle talk of art (mimesis) as "mysterious" and "inscrutable to human intelligence"?[20]

The answer lies I believe in the way that "art dwells with the same objects as chance… chance is beloved of art and art of chance".[21]

The role of chance in creative imitation is obvious when we think about the difference between an art work and a forgery of course—the latter is an attempt to produce an exact copy of an 'original', excluding chance. Yet the emphasis placed upon originality in modern culture is deeply problematic. In contrast to traditional "anachronic art" eg icons, etc, the twentieth century avant-garde both worshipped original art works, and sought within mechanical processes methods to overcome the excessive intentionality of individual commissions and the cult of personality.[22] Attempts to artificially simulate the role that chance plays in directed work is one of the lasting legacies of Surrealism and Dada. Games such as *Exquisite Corpse* imitate some of the rhythmic movement of imagination, in an attempt to introduce chance into dialogue. In late twentieth century architectural culture, the directed character of design work—its commissioned nature and civic character—was often abandoned in favour of formalistic method and aesthetics, and thus emancipated from the creative tension between intention and chance. Constant's *New Babylon* project (1959–1974) sought to try to artificially imitate the effects of historical change and chance upon the design of cities based on *freedom from* typical situations.[23] Colin Rowe's picturesque and formalistic use of Lévi-Strauss' term "bricolage" introduced faux-vernacular complexity into architecture[24] as an aesthetics of chance bereft of political *agon*.[25] Both Constant and Rowe worshipped a sort of automatic

Study models of new bell tower for Barking Abbey

---

19 Bernasconi, Robert, ed, *The Relevance of the Beautiful and Other Essays*, trans Nicholas Warner, Cambridge: Cambridge University Press, 1986, p 104 (cited by Vesely in *Architecture in the Age of Divided Representation*, p 288).

20 Vesely, *Architecture in the Age of Divided Representation*, p 287. Vesely is citing Aristotle, *Physics*, 196b5.

21 Vesely, *Architecture in the Age of Divided Representation* Vesely is citing Aristotle, *Niomachean Ethics*, 1140a20.

22 Wood, Christopher, and Alexander Nagel, *Anachronic Renaissance*, Zone Books, 2010.

23 "It is obvious that a person free to use his time for the whole of his life, free to go where he wants, when he wants, cannot make the greatest use of his freedom in a world ruled by the clock and the imperative of a fixed abode. As a way of life Homo Ludens will demand, firstly, that he responds to his need for playing, for adventure, for mobility, as well as all the conditions that facilitate the free creation of his own life. Until then, the principal activity of man had been the exploration of his natural surroundings. Homo Ludens himself will seek to transform, to recreate, those surroundings, that world, according to his new needs. The exploration and creation of the environment will them happen to coincide because, in creating his domain to explore, Homo Ludens will apply himself to exploring his own creation. Thus we will be present at an uninterrupted process of creation and re-creation, sustained by a generalised creativity that is manifested in all domains of activity", *New Babylon—A Nomadic City*, Constant Nieuwenhuys, exhibition catalogue, the Haags Gemeetenmuseum, Hague, 1974.

24 Rowe, Colin and Fred Koetter, *Collage City*, MIT, 1978. The picturesque and formalist character of their adoption of the term is clear in this passage, where Rome is described as "a collision of palaces… an anthology of closed compositions and ad hoc stuff in-between which is simultaneously a dialectic of ideal types plus a dialectic of ideal types with empirical context… something of the bricolage mentality at its most lavish… the physique and politics of Rome provide perhaps the most graphic example of collisive (sic.) fields and interstitial debris, there are the calmer versions of equivalent interests, which are not hard to find", p 106.

25 "A specific situation, by its relative nature, limits us to relative ends", *The Formal Basis of Modern Architecture*, PhD Dissertation, Peter Eisenman, Cambridge University, 1963; Facsimile published by Lars Muller, 2006, p 31. Instead, Eisenman claims, what matters is "form", and "total external order is our absolute", p 30. The term "form" is used in an attempt to limit and to control "individual expression", which Eisenman accepts as "legitimate", but which needs to be controlled for the sake of "the comprehensibility of the environment as a whole", p 29. Unsurprisingly, he studied Terragni's work for an absolutist regime in absolute terms.

complexity in design, complexity that imitates the historical, economic and social forces that create richness in cities. But their complexity is formal complexity only; complexity without dialectics, without political agon, without anything being at stake.

I believe, in contrast to this, that the civic character of architecture means that complexity cannot be approached in architectural design except in terms of situation and use. Yet on the whole the practical nature of situations remains obscured today by a "contemporary version of poetics often reduced to technical innovation and aesthetics", Vesely states, alerting us to the directed and representational character of design. The task of "restoring the practical nature of situations as a primary vehicle of design enables us", he claims, "to move away from inconclusive play with abstract forms and functions".[26] In other words, the problem facing us

Top
Study collage of Barking Abbey ruins with proposed new structures

Bottom
Study collage of Barking Abbey Green with proposed new museum tower

26 Vesely, *Architecture in the Age of Divided Representation.*

in contemporary design can be seen as the restoration of an idea of a poetics of praxis based upon mimesis of praxis.

Mimesis is not simply a matter of the *outward appearance* of something; mimesis, in architecture is the expression also of the decorum of situations housed *within* a facade. This depth cannot be fully grasped by either the introverted nature of functionalism on the one hand, nor the extroverted character of formalism on the other. Rather, decorum is the communication between both the interior and exterior of buildings, people and the world. We see this most clearly illustrated in the role that facades play as communicative spatial thresholds between interior and exterior rooms—indeed, the facade was itself understood as a type of space in Baroque architecture, one with poetic potential to situate activity in terms of decorum. This notion still has currency in modern architecture, I believe.[27]

Yet contemporary architects are still struggling with the idea of the facade as a legitimate aspect of architectural culture. Cino Zucchi describes this struggle in relation to modernist puritanism: "The facade is a phenomena. Architecture has turned it into a theme, only to try to sacrifice it like Abraham's son Isaac on the altar of method. But the modernist axiom of interior-exterior continuity, and the claim that they are a formal unity can only be regarded as an often misunderstood begging of the question. The facade implies arbitrariness." His conclusion is that "the constraints implied by the plan of a building are not capable of fully controlling the residual dimensional and material liberty of the surface of the external wall, in its constant aspiration to achieve the freedom of purely visual existence".[28] Visual discontinuity between interiors and exteriors need not imply a lack of spatial continuity, nor a lack of judgement about the appropriateness of the degree of difference between them. In other words, despite outward appearances, "the original relationship between *prepon* and mimetic representation reveals how close architectural representation is to mimesis".[29] In fact, Zucchi and Vesely both agree that whilst modern buildings might not immediately appear to possess mimetic characteristics, their success often lies in their evocation of an archetype. Vesely describes archetypes in terms of "paradigmatic situations",[30] whilst Zucchi refers to "a common language",[31] suggesting the continuity of decorum as a basis for architectural representation.[32]

---

27 The facade is the meeting between outside and inside = *Fasaden ar motet mellan ute och inne*, Peter Celsing, Museum of Finnish Architecture, 1992.
28 Zucchi, Cino, "Asnago Vender: Everyday Abstraction", in *Asnago Vender and the Construction of Modern Milan*, ed Adam Caruso and Helen Thomas, Zurich: GTA, 2014, pp 64–65.
29 Vesely, *Architecture in the Age of Divided Representation*, p 366.
30 "The persistence of primary symbols, especially in the field of architecture, contributes decisively to the formation of secondary symbols and finally to the formation of paradigmatic situations. Paradigmatic situations are similar in nature to institutions, deep structures, and archetypes. The role of the paradigmatic structure of a spatial situation is comparable to poetic mythos in a poem or a play. Both have the power to organise individual events and elements of praxis into a synthesis and give them a higher and more universal meaning." Vesely, *Architecture in the Age of Divided Representation*, p 368.
31 "In their designs, Asnago Vender did not seek a mimetic relationship with existing buildings that had a direct figurative connection. Sometimes the character of a project can be discerned through what looks like a reflection on the archetype." Zucchi, "Asnago Vender: Everyday Abstraction", p 67.
32 "But what is needed, is in my view, not a theory of decorated sheds. Rather, it is a theory which concerns itself at least in part with contemporary variants of the traditional concept of 'decorum'... to establish systems of propriety in the employment of any particular architectural vocabulary. Now, calling for the return of such a classical concept of decorum may seem even more contentious than the claims of Venturi, Scott Brown and Izenour have made that I have criticised, but I don't think that it ought to be. To begin, I should state that I can only imagine the contemporary theory of decorum being formulated in the context of the (wary) attitude manifest in a familiar remark of Jean Cocteau: 'Tact in audacity, consists in knowing how too far you can go.' Any modern theory of decorum would have to sustain that degree of ironic resonance." Baird, George, "A Critical Reflection on the Theory and Practice of Architectural Symbolism in the Work of Venturi, Rauch, and Scott Brown, and their Colleagues", 1976, in *Writings on Architecture and the City*, Artifice books on architecture, 2015.

Top
Photograph of the town crest of Barking

Middle and bottom
Model photographs of proposed museum tower 1/50 scale model with carvings by Hilary Koob-Sassen

Johan Celsing recently prefaced an essay on the continuing relevance of decorum citing Alberti—"The greatest glory in the art of building is to know what is appropriate"[33]—claiming: "that what makes a project beautiful or important cannot solely be found in the aesthetic categories is becoming increasingly clear.... Decorum therefore decouples to some extent the question of appearance from what we like personally. What is fitting can obviously take many different forms, provided that it serves the purpose demanded by the task.... Developing one's judgement to enable understanding of what is fitting, just or appropriate in an architectonic commission is the central task for every architect and, in my opinion, every individual. Judgement is trained naturally in the concrete task that we are given to solve."[34]

In architectural terms, decorum determines the dramatic character of situations and of their narrative and spatial continuity, as well as their communicative or civic role.

The pleasure of appropriateness involves patience and enjoyment in looking and thinking: "It implies that order is represented in such a way that it becomes conspicuous and actually present in sensuous abundance."[35]

It is tempting to construe Vesely's phrase "*sensuous abundance*" as inappropriate or hedonistic decoration, but I believe that these aesthetic terms, with their overtones of puritan disgust for the playful nature of reason, disguise the carnal and imaginative character of mimetic order—its superabundance of sense and sensibility.

Poetic abundance isn't an overload of information or an excess of stuff—it is an abundance of pleasure in the haptic qualities of language and the mimetic character of imagination.

For architects, this *mimetic order* resides in the "sensuous abundance" of drawing and model-making and in craft in general—there is a direct relationship between the pleasure and skill of work in the design studio, and the poetic quality of a finished building. This connection is possible because design involves the tensions and "reciprocity of the actual and the

33 Alberti, Leon Battista, *On the Art of Building in Ten Books*, trans J Rykwert, N Leach and R Tavenor, MIT, 1990.
34 Celsing, Johan, "Decorum, tentative notes on its contemporary relevance and use", unpublished essay, 2013.
35 Vesely, *Architecture in the Age of Divided Representation*, p 366.

Axonometric and study collage of proposals for Barking Abbey ruins during a summer wedding

possible... the reciprocity of necessity and freedom, where 'necessity' represents a given reality—the inevitable, necessary condition of our freedom and creativity".[36]

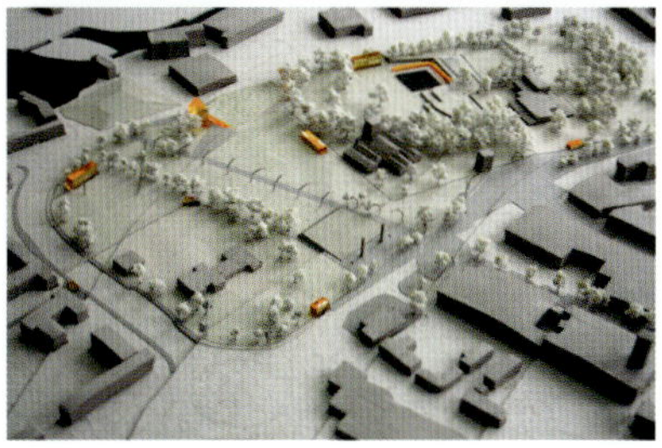

I find that *the reciprocity between freedom and necessity* comes to appearance most readily in the role that chance plays in the act of designing. Chance introduces spontaneity, whilst keeping alive the playful and directed character of design thinking, "the rhythm and movement of the processes of making itself".[37] Physical gestures and rhythms abound in model-making and drawing, uniting design with imaginative occupation, enabling the imitation and anticipation of inhabitation. In this way, the poetics of architecture co-exists as a space and time of reflection within the process of design of buildings, and has its shadow, or other, in the lag between surprise, recognition and delight, in your experiences of them. This suggests to me that the mimetic character of imagination has its shadow in the creative action of understanding the world in general—and what is at stake in both of these experiences is participation. Mimesis might be described as a form of imaginative participation.

Hans-Georg Gadamer points out that participation lies at the heart of Plato's demonstration of the beautiful—as that which is visible to all. The beautiful "finds its concrete form in the concept of participation (*methexis*) and concerns both the relation of the appearance to an idea and the relation of ideas to one another".[38] For Gadamer, participation is most evident in festivals, and indeed all art is essentially festive for him.[39]

Whilst it is tempting to see cities made up of historical building types—and the temptation for a literate architect is to want to copy these in the name of tradition or irony—a city might be best understood as a series of settings for dialogue, sites for the festive and everyday rhythms and spontaneity of city life. There is a paradox here of course. "However much beauty might be experienced as the reflection of something supraterrestial, it is still there in the visible world", Gadamer explains, and "beauty has the most important ontological function: that of mediating between idea and appearance". Yet "the beautiful appears not only in what is visibly present to the senses", Gadamer claims, because "it does so in such a way that it really exists only

---

36 Vesely, *Architecture in the Age of Divided Representation*, p 58.
37 Vesely, *Architecture in the Age of Divided Representation*, p 288.
38 Gadamer, Hans-Georg, *Truth and Method*, London: Sheed and Ward, 1993, p 481.
39 *The Relevance of the Beautiful: Art as Play, Symbol and Festival and other essays.*

Model photograph and study collage of Barking Abbey Green showing children's playground, museum tower and cafe

through it—ie emerges out of a whole".[40] Whilst "Plato linked the idea of the beautiful to that of the good, he was still aware of the difference between the two and this difference involves the *special advantage of the beautiful*", Gadamer declares.[41] The advantage it has is that: "The beautiful is distinguished from the absolutely intangible good in that it can be grasped. It is part of its own nature to be something visibly manifest. The beautiful reveals itself in the search for the good."[42]

Whilst beauty is manifest in material things, it is better, Gadamer suggests, to describe it "not as simply symmetry but appearance itself... related to the idea of 'shining'.... Beauty has a mode of being of *light*."[43] Because it is "what is 'most radiant' (*to ekphanestaton*)", Gadamer suggests, beauty is something that illuminates and makes beautiful the things that surround it.[44]

This image of beauty, or rather of *the effect of beauty*, as radiant light, evokes a force connecting and illuminating things in time and across "epochs", suggesting also something like Auerbach's sense of "flow" or *influence*. In architectural terms, this phenomenon can be seen in the influence that ideas have across different societies and their presence in buildings of different styles. It is most clearly manifest in the combined effect of buildings that are designed to sit beside each other, and, I believe, lingers in the resulting sensation that we encounter in this situation, of new things that appear both strange and familiar at once.[45]

The most explicit example of an attempt to visually represent the continuing influence of iconological themes across time is Aby Warburg's *Mnemosyne Atlas*. Begun in 1924 and incomplete at his death in 1929, it consists of 63 wooden panels 1.5 x 2 metres wrapped in black cloth, arranged thematically in 14 sections, onto which Warburg juxtaposed over 1,000 photographs of images of antique artefacts with examples of their influence upon post-Renaissance Western culture, what he called "antiquity's afterlife".[46] Christopher Johnson claims that the "*Bilderatlas* functions cartographically too, as it explores how meanings are constituted by the movement or translation of themes and styles between east and west, north and south."[47] For him, "Warburg's Atlas explores a middle way between literature and science as it makes visible patterns claiming both imaginative and referential meaning."[48] Warburg believed that the encounter of reason and emotion in artistic influence typified the role that memory (*Mnemosyne)* plays in culture generally, and his Atlas "hoped to create 'metaphoric distance'... *Distanz* that would mediate between unbridled pathos and constricting abstraction", Johnson claims. Warburg saw the perils of unmediated appropriation of the

Photographs of the new playground by Lynch Architects at Barking Abbey Green

40 Gadamer, *Truth and Method*, p 482.
41 Gadamer, *Truth and Method*, p 480.
42 Gadamer, *Truth and Method*, p 481.
43 Gadamer, *Truth and Method*.
44 Gadamer, *Truth and Method*.
45 Johnson, Christopher D, *Memory, Metaphor, and Aby Warburg's Atlas of Images*, Cornell, 2012: "Memory, Hölderlin intimates, sets us an impossible task in part because we are forever shuttling between the familiar and 'the foreign'", p 2. See also, Michaud, Philippe-Alain, *Aby Warburg and the Image in Motion*, Zone Books/MIT, 2007. A similar contemporary project, Gerhard Richter's *Atlas*, Thames and Hudson, 2007, is discussed by Teju Cole along with recent artistic projects that consider the possibilities of Richter's *Atlas Micromega*, 1962–2013, alongside Dina Kelberman's film project *I am Google*, which he describes as "less Warburg than Walmart", Cole, Teju, *The Atlas of Affect*, 7 July 2014: http://thenewinquiry.com/blogs/dtake/the-atlas-of-affect/..
46 "Preface", p x. The 63 panels of *Mnemosyne Atlas* and are grouped under these 14 thematic or "iconological" headings: 1 Coordinates of memory; 2 Astrology and mythology; 3 Archaeological models; 4 Migrations of the ancient gods; 5 Vehicles of tradition; 6 Irruption of antiquity; 7 Dionysiac formulae of emotions; 8 Nike and Fortuna; 9 From the Muses to Manet; 10 Dürer: the gods go North; 11 The age of Neptune; 12 "Art officiel" and the baroque; 13 Re-emergence of antiquity; 14 The classical tradition today. Images of Warburg's *Mnemosyne Atlas* can be seen here: http://www.engramma.it/eOS2/atlante/#
47 "Preface", p 10.
48 "Preface", p 11.

imagery of antiquity in his own lifetime "in the rise of fascism", Johnson declares, "whose imagery Warburg described as dangerously without any 'metaphoric distance' or mediation".[49] He suggests that *Mnemosyne Atlas*, was "audacious" and "perilous". Audacious because it represents "intellectual, spiritual thirst for syncretic solutions... never yields to the strictures (or rigours) of a single system of thought, never embraces the comforts of teleology, and yet continuously tries to expand the compass, the discipline of boundaries, of its questions. Perilous because his historical enquiries are fuelled by a precarious ideal affirming that the polar forces of reason and unreason can be balanced in ways redemptive not only for an individual thinker beset by personal demons, or *monstra*, as Warburg came to call them, but also the culture in which one labours and whose origins, history and future compel contemplation."[50] Warburg attempted to reunite the ethical and the aesthetic aspects of culture in a "*Denkraum*" or "thought-space", made up of his selection of wordless images—"ghost stories for all adults"[51]—that illustrate the power of metaphor across cultures, "anchored in the contingencies of language, personality, and ethics".[52] Johnson states that "for Warburg, metaphor is both the means (vehicle) and the aim (tenor) of his 'dialectic of the monster', the name he gives to the cognitive and historical process by which the artist, cosmographer, and critical spectator mediate between numerous polarities—world and self, fear and serenity, past and present, religion and science, magic and reason, the *vita activa* and the *vita contemplativa*, ecstasy and melancholy, and above all word and image—that they may yield phenomenological knowledge, psychological balance, and however tenuously, historical understanding. In brief, *Mnemosyne*'s panels show when and how metaphor (or 'pathos formula' or 'dynamoram') wins and loses a connection with what Edmund Husserl and Hans Blumenberg term the 'lifeworld'."[53] Warburg's emphasis upon the role of metaphor in imagination and memory suggests the inherently mimetic character of both. The tacit role that mimesis plays in daily life, and in the imagination, reveals its profound and continuing modest potency and relevance today.

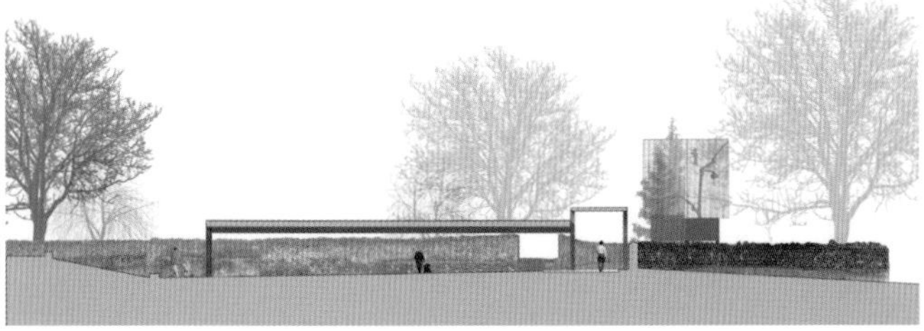

Top
Collage study of Lynch Architects' proposals for Barking Abbey Ruins showing the synchronicity of seasons and its everyday and festive use as part of the town

Above
Site sections through Barking Abbey Ruins showing our proposals for "mimetic" structures

49 "Preface", p 12.
50 "Preface", p 13.
51 Warburg, Aby, *Mnemosyne: Grundbegriffe I*, fol 3, WIA, III.102.3.3.
52 "Preface", p 13.
53 "Preface", p x.

Addendum:
Notes on Mimesis and Type at Barking Abbey Green and The ELBWO Centre

ELBWO is an impure archetype. A collage of a typical West Indian yard house type based on a long veranda, and also something contextual: contextual not only to the client but also to the site typology. The setting was a courtyard defined by a line of south-facing mature trees in front of a Victorian, brick, Methodist chapel. This at least was our reading of the situation, of something occluded and lacking a cloister or any mediation between an obdurate windowless form and the courtyard and the world beyond.
Our design response was at once a high cultural archetype, ie a loggia, and also something typical and highly culturally specific, ie a verandah.

It is important to recognise that the design was in a very particular place and for an unusually cohesive range of uses and users, eg a black women's group operating as a crèche and an informal cultural centre as well as a local community hall.

The whole thing came to life as soon as it opened in summer 2004, people sitting on the verandah steps in the midday shade of the trees, seemingly naturally, etc.

Barking extends the logic of this empathetic and mimetic approach to site, use and history, recreating ghosts of the destroyed cloisters and religious structures around the ruined abbey, marking out spaces by traces of architectonic presence. For example, the *Hortus Conclusis* would be defined by shadows of colonnades around its edge, the metal columns framing modern versions of ambulatory routes, describing what is missing rather than replacing or directly reproducing what is lost.

These new structures house ramps and provide artificial lighting, making the site accessible physically; whilst also acting as interpretative structures for heuristic educational purposes. The phantom colonnades accommodate everyday uses and amplify the civic significance of the site, providing facilities for school visits and creating shelter for permanent exhibits of artefacts and historical information.

The various archetypes form something like a memory atlas. They also describe something that is hardly there, and are an attempt to demarcate and bring to the surface ancient spatial relationships that defined the site as sacred and semi-sacred territories. Our aim in trying to do this is educational and cultural—making visible the reasons why the ruin is an important historical artefact itself as a piece of semi-visible architecture territory.

We are also trying to find ways to support the continuing religious use of the site for summer weddings and for an orthodox pilgrimage each spring (there are lots of immigrants in Essex and the abbey is pre-schism so acts as a pilgrimage site for all Christians to worship the same saints, acknowledging its role as a popular centre of national reconciliation and universal identity).

Our new structures enable the site to be used in a mundane sense everyday, as we provide safe access across the ruins connecting the riverside to the town centre.

Our strategy for Barking Abbey Green was to have had the status of a master plan delineating and limiting a development strategy for the river edge, limiting future development of yet more "out of town" shopping sheds further cutting the town off from nature.

Studies and model photographs of proposals for Barking Abbey Green and the ruins of the Abbey

In these restorative projects architectural types are bound up with memory, creative mimesis, practical circumstances and cultural continuity—suggesting that they are exemplary generally of the ways in which we encounter communicative elements in our work as architects.

William Blake seemed to understand very well the difficult task of communicating in imaginative work, suggesting that the artistic problem of knowing when to stop is also a question of energy and risk: “You never know what is enough unless you know what is more than enough”.

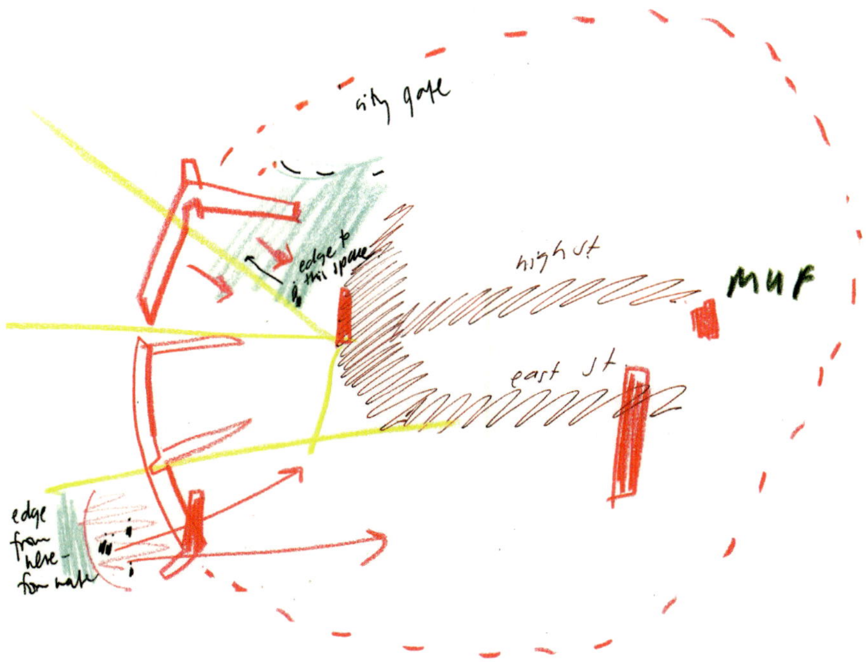

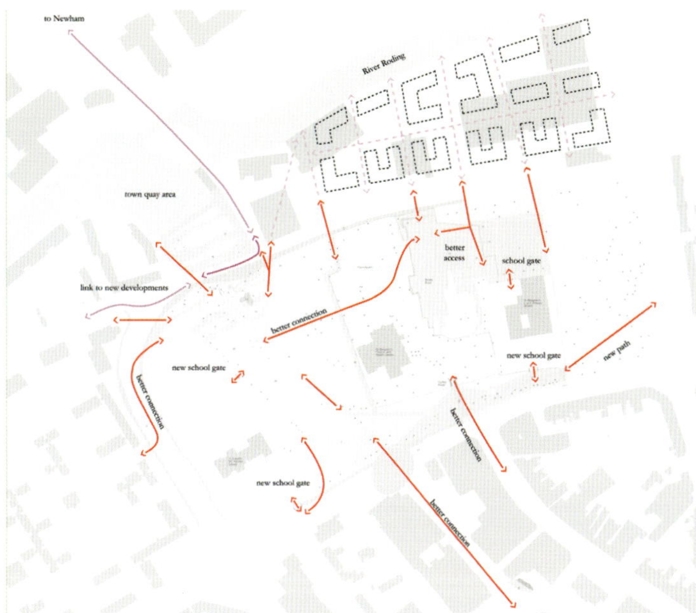

Links and Connections

- better connections
- redirected route for cars
- possible future connections to river
- possible future mixed-use scheme established by routes to river

Initial study sketch for Barking Abbey Green showing the concept of a ‘broken city wall’ made up of fragments of historic types and the final masterplan site plan drawing

ZONE

Index

Current and Past Staff
Directors: Patrick Lynch, Claudia Lynch, David Evans
Associate Director: Rachel Elliot
Associates: Laura Evans, Carol James, Sandra Martin, Luke McDonald

Rory Allen, Enrico Arrigoni, Gunvor Bakke Kvinlog, Filipa Botello, Kieran Brash, Maia Caiger-Smith, Doug Carson, Dado Celikovic, Mary Chapman, Ciaran Chapple-Canty, Samuel Chisholm, Mike Clancy, Chiara Codoni, Alessia Colombo, Valentina Colombo, Ewan Cooper, Christian Cuninghame, Jacques Dahan, Rachel Delargey, Clémence Devictor-Monk, Laura Dietsch, Ultan Donagher, Brendan Durkin, Jenny Ersson, Nicola Finlay, Eleanor Grierson, Michael Gollings, Joana Gonçalves, Lorenzo Guzzini, Laura Haenni, Gavin Henneberry, Jessica Hendey, Emilia Herman, Andrew Jackson, Gwilym Jones, Oliver Juggins, Chris Knight, Andrew Laurie, Rogelio Lema, Brenda Leonard, Myran Lynch-Bathgate, Philip Lyons, Dan Marcal, Matthew McCrum, Deirdre McKenna, Adrian McGeehan, Caoilinn McConville, Elaine McQuaid, Eleni Makri, Douglas Murphy, Eoin Murphy, Paul Nicholson, Markus Nurkkala, Katie O'Connell, Nicola Osbourne, Colin O'Sullivan, Sara Oxley, Suzi Pain, Zoe Panayi, Payal Patel, Enrico Pistocchi, Hugh Queenan, Sophie Roycroft, Naomi Shaw, Matthew Shepherd, Hannah Schneebeli, Katrin Sölter, Paulo Sousa, Chris Storie, Ben Strak, Karin Templin, Lara Vettorato, Madelena Vidigal, Nadine Wagner, Antje Weihen, Nathaniel Welham, Matt Wells, Richard Yates and Pete Youthed.

Acknowledgements
Special thanks to David Grandorge for his photographs and inspirational commentary, and to Laura Evans, Eleanor Grierson and Ben Strak for the production of drawings for this book. Thanks to Duncan McCorquodale for his help and guidance in formulating and editing this publication. It perhaps doesn't need to be said how much this work is inspired by, and is dedicated to, the fond memory of absent friends.

Image Credits
Unless stated all other images are by Patrick Lynch or Lynch architects.
All reasonable efforts have been made to trace the copyright holders of images.

Rory Allen: pp 73, 186 (bottom left)
Sue Barr: pp 26, 28, 34, 36, 40, 86, 201, 203
Hèlene Binet: p 49
Christian Cuninghame: pp 58, 61 (bottom row), 62 (top right), 64–68
David Evans: pp 17, 150 (top left), 181
Chris Gasgoine: p 91
David Grandorge: pp 19, 25, 29, 32, 35, 37–39, 41–43, 46, 48, 62 (top left), 75, 77, 79, 84, 102, 104, 106, 108–111, 137, 162–169, 171, 174, 176, 177 (bottom right), 178, 179, 181–185, 187, 190, 191, 220, 221
Julia Grassi: pp 44, 45
Miller Hare: p 127
Carol James: p 180
Andy Laurie: p 62 (bottom right)
Claudia Lynch: p 186 (bottom right)
Luke McDonald: p 190 (top left and bottom right)
Karin Templin: p 116
Paulo Sousa: p 186 (top left)
Morley Von Sternberg: pp 82, 83, 88, 89, 90
Luke White: p 47

Artifice books on architecture
10A Acton Street
London
WC1X 9NG

t. +44 (0)207 713 5097
f. +44 (0)207 713 8682
sales@artificebooksonline.com
www.artificebooksonline.com

Designed by João Mota and Albino Tavares at Artifice books on architecture.

British Library Cataloguing-in-Publication Data.
A CIP record for this book is available from the British Library.

ISBN 978 1 908967 66 4

Artifice books on architecture is an environmentally responsible company.
mimesis: Lynch Architects is printed on sustainably sourced paper.

Artifice
books on architecture